PROJECT BASED LEARNING FOR THE AUSTRALIAN CURRICULUM

ARE HUMANS WILD AT HEART?

AND OTHER EPIC ENGLISH PROJECTS FOR YEARS 9–10

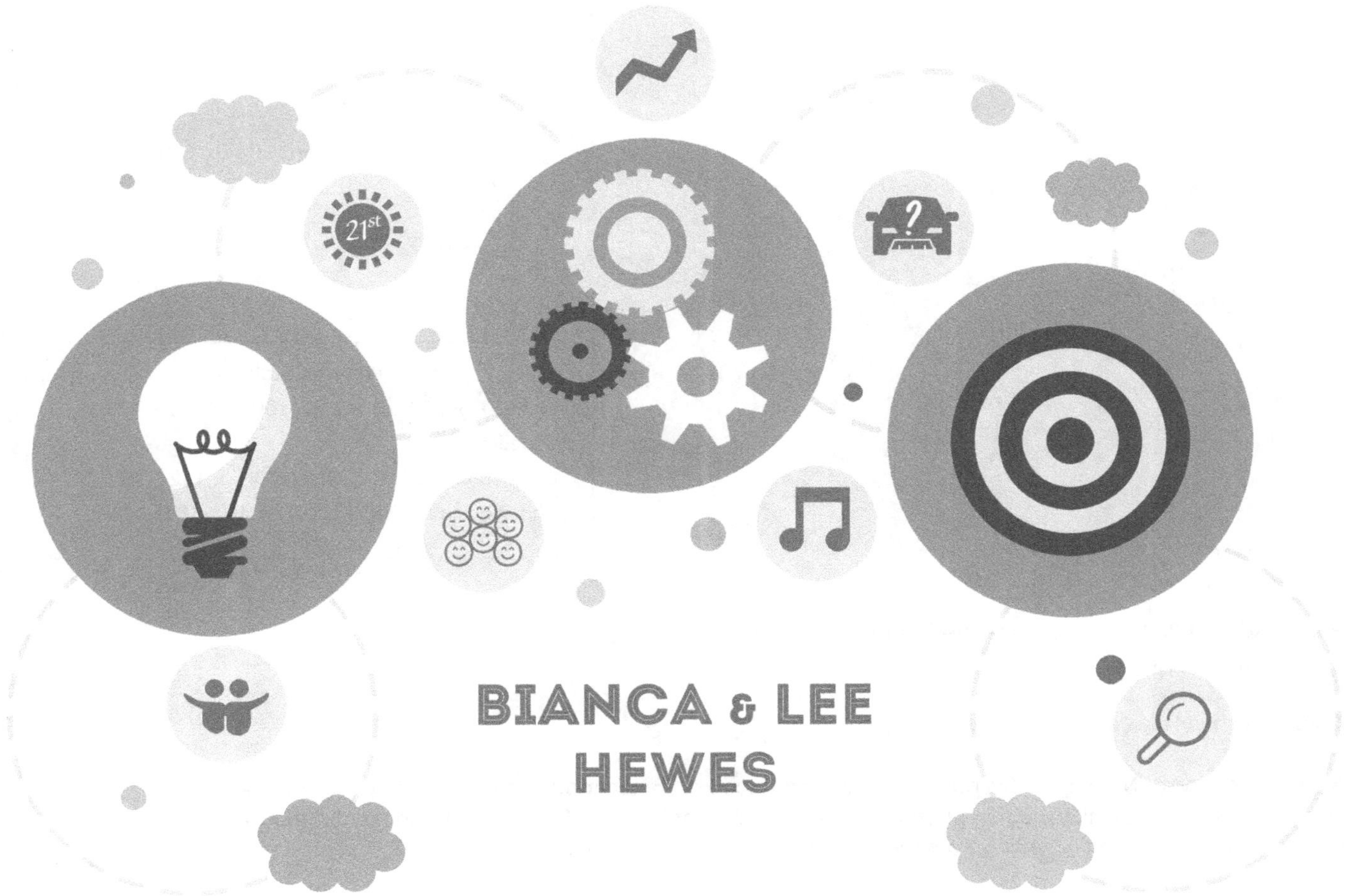

BIANCA & LEE HEWES

amba press

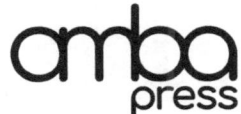

Picture Credits
iStock: 20, 36, 62, 70, 83, 87, 100, 116, 124, 125
Wikipedia: 21
Freepik.com: vi, 21, 27, 33, 57, 70, 75, 132, 139
Author's own pictures: 13, 14, 25, 108, 141–144

Published in 2025 by Amba Press, Melbourne, Australia
www.ambapress.com.au

© 2025 Bianca Hewes and Lee Hewes

All rights reserved. No part of this book may be reproduced or transmitted in any form or by any means, electronic or mechanical, including photocopying, recording or by any information storage and retrieval system, without prior permission in writing from the publisher.

Previously published in 2016 by Hawker Brownlow Education.
This edition replaces all previous editions.

ISBN: 9781923403024 (pbk)
ISBN: 9781923403031 (ebk)

A catalogue record for this book is available from the National Library of Australia.

CONTENTS

Image Credits — ii
How to Use This Book — v

Part One: The What, Why and How of Project Based Learning — 1

Part Two: Sample Projects — 17

Year 9 projects:

1. Mad Blood — 19
   - Driving Question: What can we learn from tragedy?
   - Type of Text: Persuasive (personal essay) and imaginative texts (play/performance)

2. Mobile Learning — 35
   - Driving Question: How can mobile phones be used to help us learn in high school?
   - Type of Text: Persuasive (speech)

3. Speak Up — 47
   - Driving Question: How can one voice change the world?
   - Type of Text: Informative (analytical essay), imaginative (poetry)

4. Teens Unite — 61
   - Driving Question: How can we support teenagers who are finding life hard?
   - Type of Text: Informative (report), persuasive (visual rep), imaginative (novel)

5. Midnight Snacks — 69
   - Driving Question: How can we compose a fantasy story that will interest eight-year-olds?
   - Type of Text: Informative (report) and imaginative (short story)

Year 10 projects:

1. Emotional Excess — 81
   - Driving Question: Why do emos write poetry?
   - Type of Text: Informative (essay and podcast), imaginative (poetry)

2. More Than Meets the Eye — 99
   - Driving Question: What makes a story worth stealing?
   - Type of Text: Informative (literary essay) and imaginative (fan fiction)

3. Something Wicked   115
   - Driving Question: How can we design a winning advertising campaign for a production of Macbeth?
   - Type of Text: Persuasive (advertising campaign) and imaginative (play)

4. Wild At Heart   137
   - Driving Question: Are humans wild at heart?
   - Type of Text: Informative (personal essay) and imaginative (picture book and film)

5. English Composition Project – ECP   153
   - Driving Question: Students generate their own driving questions
   - Type of Text: Informative (research report), imaginative OR persuasive (ECP)

Part Three: Additional Resources   159

HOW TO USE THIS BOOK

This book has been designed to support you as you begin experimenting with Project Based Learning (PBL) in your English classroom. Of course, the methodology of PBL is relevant to areas other than English — it can be used in a range of subjects, with many projects actually integrating more than one subject across the curriculum. Trying out something new in the classroom is always a daunting experience because feedback on success or failure is immediate. The great thing about PBL is that it is creative for both the teacher and the student, and that means that experimentation, and sometimes failure, is a natural part of the process.

This book has been structured into three distinct parts, designed to help you feel supported in your PBL journey.

PART ONE: THE WHAT, WHY AND HOW OF PROJECT BASED LEARNING

The first part of the book provides you with some background information about the nature and purpose of PBL, as well as outlining key strategies to ensure a successful and enjoyable learning experience for you and your students. This section also includes a discussion of how assessment works in PBL, as well as the relationship between PBL and the Australian Curriculum's General Capabilities.

PART TWO: SAMPLE PROJECTS

The second part of the book provides you with a selection of sample projects suitable for students in Years 9 and 10. You will be pleasantly surprised that a lot of the activities in this section look familiar — that's because PBL is about taking the best teaching strategies and re-purposing them. The difference with PBL is that it empowers students to see a purpose for their learning beyond the classroom and to feel confident that they know where they are headed while they move through the project process.

Each project includes the following:
- Driving question
- Project outline
- Summary of learning experiences
- Literacy focus
- Specific mode(s) and text form(s)
- 21st-century skills
- Assessment strategies
- A range of resources to support learning

For both Years 9 and 10, there are two very detailed projects. We have given you a week-by-week outline of how the projects can be run with your students, as well as providing useful resources to support implementation of your first projects. Once you have implemented a couple of projects, and you begin to feel more confident with PBL, the remaining projects will act as loose guides. These projects are much less detailed, allowing you more scope to adapt and develop them to suit your students' needs and interests.

NOTE: It is essential that you adapt the given projects to make them meet the needs and interests of your students. Central to effective PBL is student ownership of learning and this can only be achieved if students feel that the project is relevant to their experiences and context. What may be considered significant and relevant to students on Sydney's northern beaches may have no relevance to students from Broome, Western Australia.

PART THREE: ADDITIONAL RESOURCES

The third part of the book is full of extra resources to help you design and run your own engaging projects for your English classes.

NOTE: Throughout this book you will see the icons below. These will help you to navigate the projects and easily identify the key content and elements of each project.

DRIVING QUESTION

DISCOVER

CREATE

SHARE

ASSESSMENT

21ST CENTURY SKILLS

FORMATIVE ASSESSMENT

PART ONE
THE WHAT, WHY AND HOW OF PROJECT BASED LEARNING

WHAT IS PROJECT BASED LEARNING (PBL)?

Project Based Learning is an inquiry-driven methodology that engages students in relevant, real-world problems that require them to attain and strengthen skills essential for success in the 21st century – collaboration, communication, creativity and digital citizenship.

The highly successful PBL approach outlined in our book has been developed over the last several years in the context of Australian primary and secondary schools. This is not to say, however, that the approach would not be useful in any other context. Our PBL approach is characterised by three interconnected learning stages: Discover, Create and Share. This process sees teachers and students inquire into a particular topic (Discover) and create a product (Create) to be shared with an authentic audience (Share). We feel that this structure gives students support as they move through a project and that the overarching approach authentically reflects the design and composition process undertaken by individuals working in creative fields relevant to the study of English. Creating products for an outside audience necessitates that students solve problems that have implications for the world outside of the classroom. Students need to consider to whom they are pitching their product or ideas, in which medium and how to best reach that audience in order to design something that will be of value to them.

During PBL, students may work individually or in a small team, depending on the nature of the project. The ideal team size is four students, as this allows every student to have an opportunity to contribute meaningfully to project work. The duration of a project will vary, depending on the nature of the inquiry and the composition. We have found that shorter projects are effective when you're first introducing PBL to your students. The projects in this book range from four weeks to six weeks in length. If a project is too long, you risk students becoming disengaged.

The role of the teacher is different in a PBL classroom to that of a teacher in an exclusively teacher-centred classroom. Your role will change throughout the different stages of the project. The majority of the time you will be there to support student learning by working closely with students individually or in small groups. There will be times where you will teach in a more traditional teacher-centred style, especially when you're introducing project requirements or instructing the whole class on important content or skills. PBL teachers must be very flexible and keep a close eye on students' learning to ensure that you can support their needs 'just in time'.

It's important at this early stage to point out that PBL is not the same as 'doing a project'. Traditionally, school projects come at the end of a unit of work in the form of some type of artefact that students must create – at home, and often with the assistance of their parents – to demonstrate what they have learned. Obvious examples of these are cardboard posters about Shakespeare's life, a clay pyramid, a model of the solar system or an 'ancient' parchment made with old tea bags. These objects are submitted to the teacher with the purpose of being assessed. With PBL the project does not come at the end of learning – it is the learning. The focus is on how students discover content and develop skills through the process of inquiry, in class and with the full support of their teacher, in order to create something or present something to a public audience.

PBL typically contains several fundamental components, outlined in the '**HOW DOES PBL RUN IN THE ENGLISH CLASSROOM?**' section, with detailed examples given throughout the course of the book.

WHY ENGLISH TEACHERS SHOULD CARE ABOUT PBL: INTEGRATING MULTI-LITERACIES, FORMATIVE ASSESSMENT AND DIGITAL TECHNOLOGIES

There is impetus for pedagogical change in the English classroom. This impetus stems from our rapidly changing world, as observed by Bull and Anstey (2010, p.6): 'Literacy teaching and learning should respond to the rapid changes in literacy arising from increasing globalisation, technology and social diversity.' This transforming social, cultural and technological landscape necessarily influences the responsibilities of the secondary English teacher in Australia and brings with it a set of new challenges. Three of these challenges are the purposeful integration of digital technologies into the classroom, the nature of assessment and the necessity of teaching multi-literacies. It can be argued that these challenges may be successfully overcome by the reshaping of traditional teacher-centred pedagogy in the Australian secondary English classroom to a more student-centred and inquiry-based pedagogy. In fact, this impetus toward pedagogical change is reflected in the new Australian Curriculum: English.

Over the last ten years, English teachers have increasingly faced the challenge of when, how and why to introduce digital technologies into their lessons. Moreover, the Australian Curriculum: English stipulates that teachers are required to help students to become productive, creative and confident users of technology. The types of digital technologies that are beginning to be seen in educational settings include a combination of fixed (televisions, Interactive Whiteboards [IWBs], computer lab) and mobile technologies (iPads, iPods, mobile phones) as well as the software and web-based tools teachers and students access. Digital technologies that teachers and students bring into the English classroom should be meaningfully integrated into learning activities.

A second challenge faced by secondary English teachers in Australia is the nature of assessment. Often the primary assessment in English is summative despite evidence that formative assessment for learning practices has 'more impact on learning than any other general factor' (Petty, 2006). The Australian Curriculum: English advocates assessment for learning practices including peer- and self-assessment. In their seminal paper, Black and Wiliam (1998) conclude that the introduction of effective assessment for learning 'will require significant changes in classroom practice' (p. 141) because 'instruction and formative assessment are indivisible' (p. 143). Importantly, Black and William propose that 'what is needed is a classroom culture of questioning and deep thinking, in which pupils learn from discussions with teachers and peers' (p. 146). These features are key elements of project-based pedagogies that have been shown to 'have documented positive changes for teachers and students in motivation, attitude toward learning, and skills, including work habits, critical thinking skills and problem-solving' (Barron and Darling-Hammond, p. 4, 2008).

The final challenge facing English teachers today is the necessity of teaching multi-literacies. The term multi-literacies was coined by the New London Group and is defined as 'a new approach to literacy teaching [that] overcomes the limitations of traditional approaches by emphasising how negotiating the multiple linguistic and cultural differences in our society is central to the pragmatics of the working, civic, and private lives of students'. A three-year ethnographic study by Ito et al (2008) describes how 'new media allow for a degree of freedom and autonomy for youth that is less apparent in a classroom setting (p. 2)' and conclude that 'the diversity in forms of literacy (accessed by young people) means it is problematic to develop a standardised set of benchmarks to measure' (p. 2) multi-literacies. Traditionally English in Australia has been viewed as a teacher-centred discipline with a heavy focus on linguistic literacy – reading and writing. However the introduction of multi-modal and multimedia texts into the Australian Curriculum: English reshapes our understanding of the English subject. English teachers are now responsible for the teaching of multi-literacies, inviting another challenge for teachers because 'literacy must address the impact of new communication technologies, and the texts delivered by them' (Bull and Anstey, 2010, p. 6).

Meeting the demands of changing literacy needs, curriculum changes and the federal 1–1 initiative forces secondary English teachers in Australia to reconsider their pedagogy. One methodology that may provide teachers with a scaffold to integrate digital technologies and multi-literacies into the English classroom is Project Based Learning (PBL). This humble book hopes to support English teachers as they take steps towards modifying their practice to meet the exciting, yet challenging changes with which they are confronted.

REFERENCES

Barron, B. & Darling-Hammond, L. (2008). Teaching for meaningful learning: A review of research on inquiry-based and cooperative learning. In L. Darling-Hammond, Barron, B., Pearson, D., Schoenfeld, A., Stage, E., Zimmerman, T., Cervetti, G. & Tison, J. (Ed.), *Powerful Learning: What We Know About Teaching for Understanding* (pp. 11–70). San Francisco: Jossey-Bass.

Black, P. Wiliam, D. (1998). Inside the black box: Raising standards through classroom assessment. *The Phi Delta Kappan* 80(2), 139–148.

Bull, G. Anstey, M. (2010). *Redefining Literacy and Text. Evolving pedagogies: reading and writing in a multi-modal world.* Carlton South, Vic: Education Services Australia.

Mizuko, I., Horst, H. A., Bittanti, M., Boyd, D., Herr-Stephenson, B., Lange, P. G., Pascoe, C. J., Robinson, L. . (2008). *Living and Learning with New Media: Summary of Findings from the Digital Youth Project. The John D. and Catherine T. MacArthur Foundation Reports on Digital Media and Learning,* November 2008.

PROJECT BASED LEARNING AND THE GENERAL CAPABILITIES

NOTE: *While the term 'General Capabilities' is specific to our context as Australian teachers (it comes from our national curriculum), the capabilities themselves are relevant to every teacher around the world as they are essential skills that all students must master to be successful in the 21st century.*

The Australian Curriculum clearly articulates an awareness of the need to change our perceptions of learners and our practice as teachers. This is articulated through the General Capabilities and the Cross-Curriculum Priorities. The image below presents an overview of the General Capabilities. The central text is our goal as educators for our students — for each to become a *'successful learner, confident and creative individual and active and informed citizen'*. It is our intention to show how each of the general capabilities aligns with the key elements of PBL that were identified by the Buck Institute for Education. These 8 essentials for PBL are: Voice and Choice; Significant Content; In-depth Inquiry; Public Audience; Revision & Reflection; Driving Question; Need to Know and 21st-Century Skills. Where possible we give examples of how each capability can be engaged in the PBL English classroom. It is our belief that PBL is a methodology that provides students with the opportunity to strengthen, develop and demonstrate each of these capabilities.

Adapted from: www.australiancurriculum.edu.au/GeneralCapabilities/Overview/general-capabilities-in-the-australian-curriculum

LITERACY

Literacy is the need to know for all young people. Being literate opens the door to the other capabilities. Without being literate, it's very difficult to contribute and participate meaningfully in society. It's not impossible; it's just very difficult. Remember as well that literacy includes visual literacy and critical literacy. During PBL, literacy is developed through both explicit instruction and through more constructivist, constructionist and collaborative learning strategies.

Furthermore, a key aspect of PBL is the process of planning, drafting, peer/self assessment and revision. When applied to written or spoken products, this process has a significant impact on students' literacy skills. This process becomes more pertinent for students when they are producing the product for a public audience – online or face-to-face.

NUMERACY

PBL provides students with the opportunity to think in a more open way about their subjects. The segregating of subjects is an unfortunate consequence of the traditional schooling model. Thirty minutes on a bus trip chatting with colleagues from other faculties and you'll discover wonderful connections between your subjects, such as the connections between patterns in English and Maths. The moment we stop talking about covering content and start talking real-world applications of our subjects, we realise the need to see our subjects as interrelated. When we are driven by interest and real-world application, not only does engagement improve, but so do learning outcomes.

The trend in the US at the moment is STEM – the integration of the study of Science, Technology, Engineering and Maths. Through multi-disciplinary projects, students are mastering STEM skills. Moreover, these projects drive students through a process of in-depth inquiry as they determine what they need to know and how to find out this information or develop these skills. A lot of the skills you develop by running the projects in this book can be used to design and run successful multi-disciplinary projects in your school.

Numeracy can be incorporated into English projects too. Projects may require students to conduct in-depth inquiry through surveys and analyse the data they collect. They may also engage with the data collected by others (often accessed online) and use this to support their findings about their topic. Even everyday numeracy comes into play as students estimate and calculate the amount of food and drink needed (and related costs) when planning the presentation of learning to a public audience.

PBL necessitates in-depth inquiry. A significant part of both qualitative and quantitative research is accessing numerical data – be it graphs, statistics, tables etc. This applies to all subjects. If we don't give our students the opportunity to engage with significant content through in-depth inquiry, we're missing a wonderful chance to allow them to appreciate the power and importance of numbers, and not just in Maths.

INFORMATION AND COMMUNICATION TECHNOLOGY

While PBL isn't about technology (you can easily complete a great project without access to any technology) it certainly is enhanced by access to a range of ICTs. During PBL, ICT capability develops naturally as part of the student's learning. However, it's not about learning to use a particular online tool or program just for the sake of it, or because it might make boring work a little bit more engaging. The early stage of all projects is in-depth inquiry – this is the stage where students are driven by deep and personally developed questions about the project. Like everyone in the 21st century, students will begin their research on the Internet. This phase gives teachers a wonderful opportunity to model effective research skills and the importance of curating information using a variety of online tools (social bookmarking sites and tools like Pinterest, Scoop.it are popular at this stage). Students learn these skills not because the teacher has determined they are good for them, but because they need to know them in order to be successful with their project.

Collaboration and communication are key to PBL because students spend most of their time working in small teams. We're told so often that these are the 21st-century skills for young people to master – the workforce is collaborative and globalised, therefore our students need to be able to work in a team and to communicate effectively with anyone, anywhere and at any time. This is where an online classroom is essential – not as a space where resources are accessed, but rather as a space where students can collaborate and communicate whenever they need to. Edmodo is an excellent tool for this purpose. This social network for education allows students to develop their digital citizenship (communicating with courtesy, compassion and clarity) in the eye of their teacher and they can communicate with their teams whenever they need to. Teachers can easily assess the development of these 21st-century skills and quickly give feedback to praise good behaviours and redirect negative behaviours.

ICTs play a big part in the revision and reflection process of PBL. In all projects, students are required to draft and revise their work. This process is enhanced through the use of tools like Google Docs (great for collaborative writing and planning) and more familiar programs like Microsoft Word, where students can use track changes and comments to illustrate their revisions. One of the core routines of PBL is goal-setting and reflecting on learning. This process can be done in a workbook, but it's far more effective when done using a site like Edmodo or blogs. Blogging throughout a project really allows students to appreciate that learning is a process and that improvement happens over time. Blogging gives students a place to voice both their concerns about the project as well as the joy of successfully solving a problem or creating something amazing.

Finally, the most obvious use of ICTs during PBL is for creating the product and accessing a public audience. Allowing students to have a voice and choice as part of a project is essential to ensure engagement and relevance of learning. This voice and choice typically comes into play around the product that teams will be producing to demonstrate their learning. Your students might choose from a range of forms, some including ICTs, such as videos, websites and online magazines. You might enjoy setting a challenge for your students, so they need to create a type of text they know nothing about, forcing them to develop their ICT capabilities. This can make some students uncomfortable, because they're really being pushed, but if you're there to provide support just in time then this is a great opportunity for mastering responsible risk taking. Your students will enjoy creating cool products such as websites, podcasts, short films and online fiction – things they might not normally get the opportunity to make in English.

Of course, all of these products would mean nothing if they didn't have an authentic, public audience. Teachers are time poor (and our students are too) so having access to an online audience rather than an after-school audience of mums and dads can be really helpful. One great thing to do is to connect with another class from somewhere else in the world – even if it's just the primary school forty minutes away. Today there is a range of technologies at our disposal that can facilitate this connection – Skype, Edmodo and YouTube are just a few. If connecting with another class sounds too risky for you, do a bit of networking and see if you can get a guest expert to Skype in to hear your students' final presentations. Our young people need these experiences – their learning should not be confined to the four walls of the classroom.

CRITICAL AND CREATIVE THINKING

Critical and creative thinking are life-long skills that all people should master. It's this type of thinking that can lead to a happy and successful life. Of course, teaching critical and creative thinking skills is a conundrum for teachers who feel pressured to cover a lot of content. Luckily for people using PBL as their main teaching method, critical and creative thinking is much easier to develop and refine.

As you will have noticed, the English projects in this book are broken down into three main parts: inquiry/discovery/research, create/compose/produce and present/promote. Of course, the first part of the project doesn't really stop; inquiry is an iterative process and necessary at all stages. It is important to use a lot of visible thinking strategies at all stages of PBL, as these develop and strengthen critical and creative thinking. Making your thinking visible is an important 21st-century skill. This type of thinking is new but it is extremely important in our world today as problems become more complex and more immediate. Strong critical and creative thinking is necessary if our young people are to thrive in our ridiculously fast 21st-century world. If we spend time making thinking visible – showcasing to ourselves and our peers what we're thinking, how we're thinking and why we're thinking like that about a topic, product, etc. – then we are valuing critical and creative thinking; we're having conversations about it in class. This is a way of empowering our young people to see that they *can* and *do* think this way.

Through PBL in the English classroom your students will develop their creative thinking by composing and designing products like podcasts, websites, rap battles, narrative poetry, collaborative novellas, machinima, short films and anthologies of personal essays. This process is predicated on revision and reflection. There are many visible thinking strategies for brainstorming and planning that your students can utilise. These include star-bursting, KWL tables, think/pair/share, think/puzzle/explore and mind-mapping on portable whiteboards. Another excellent creative thinking activity is whole-group 'what if' question-asking when students present plans or drafts of their work to their peers.

As previously mentioned, projects necessitate in-depth inquiry. Students are developing their critical thinking as they learn to curate information found on the Internet (and sometimes even in books). There are lots of protocols available to support students in their ability to judge the quality, credibility and relevance of information that they find on the web. PBL means that students aren't being taught these skills in a 'one-off' lesson, rather they are using these methods time and time again at the beginning stages of their projects. We need to have young people who are critical of the content that is delivered to them via the media. This is essential in a media-rich age where consumerism has become the natural state for our young people. A great activity is to actually teach students how to use Google – people expect that this knowledge and skill is a given. Another strategy that encourages critical thinking is the question-formulating technique (QFT). This is a strategy that supports students in their question-asking as they learn to identify open and closed questions and how to develop the best questions to ask. The QFT has resulted in some great questions students have made visible to their peers through writing with whiteboard markers on windows and displaying questions on the walls of the classroom.

Finally, giving students the freedom to pursue their interests in projects (even if all you feel you can allow is choice in product or audience), allows them to think more deeply about their own passions. Passions are *the* drivers of creative and critical thinking. There are a number of stages within PBL where students can be given a voice – what is the significance of the topic to their lives? what are their concerns about it? are we missing something pertinent to them as human beings? – two being the crafting of the driving question and through daily reflection on their feelings about the project and their learning. To discover student interest you could do one of these activities:

- get them to write you a letter introducing themselves to you
- get them to list the five things most important to them in their lives
- do circle time where you focus on favourite ways to learn, favourite activities or what they want to do when they leave school
- get your students passion-blogging once a week about what they value the most right now.

PERSONAL AND SOCIAL CAPABILITY

All teachers want their students to go off and live happy and successful lives. Just what successful means and looks like varies significantly between our young people. This is something that we, as teachers, need to accept. Success for many of our students is simply to be happy and healthy, to feel safe and to feel valued. This capability is great because it requires teachers to see the human being behind the student.

This is about considering how our young people are developing emotionally and socially. It's about being great role models and facilitating learning experiences that ensure these young people are being given the opportunity to develop their *self-awareness, self-management, social-awareness and social-management* (these are the four elements of Personal and Social capability as outlined in the AC document). According to the AC, if you just teach the document, students will develop all of these aspects of personal and social capability. We firmly believe that through PBL, students can most effectively develop these capabilities.

The best type of PBL is real-world and authentic. As Suzie Boss says, PBL gives students the opportunity to contribute to and change (even slightly) their world. Boss says all projects should target one of the three As: action, awareness and advocacy. Essentially, if a project is going to be significant, engaging and valuable, it will allow students to develop a sense of themselves and their role within their local and wider community. Students will work on real-world problems in their community or wider society (such as transport issues, employment, youth homelessness, environmental issues, bullying, depression etc.) and contribute to solving these problems in some way. By giving our young people a voice through them seeking a public audience for their learning, their compositions and their concerns, we are helping them to develop a better sense of themselves as active and effective contributors to their local and global communities.

ETHICAL UNDERSTANDING

According to the Australian Curriculum, 'Ethical understanding involves students in building a strong personal and socially oriented ethical outlook that helps them to manage context, conflict and uncertainty, and to develop an awareness of the influence that their values and behaviour have on others.' In high school we're often working with young people who simply lack resilience or a deep appreciation for their own values and how these can impact those around them. Why? Because they are young people finding their place within the world. But maybe it's also because they don't understand or can't appreciate the relevance of what they are doing RIGHT NOW in their school lives. To teenagers, school can often seem like they're in a holding pen waiting until they're given the chance to be morally responsible. In order to support our students to develop 'personal values and attributes such as honesty, resilience, empathy and respect for others' (*Melbourne Declaration on Education Goals for Young Australians*) we need to create learning experiences that foster and nurture these values and attributes.

PBL is about problem finding and problem solving. Not the problems in the back of the book, or the imaginary problems identified in a novel, but the REAL problems of our world that need addressing. It is in the driving question of a project that we see the centrality of problems. These problems might be based in the class (*How can we design a learning space that supports the needs of all learners?*), school (*Can we, as students, prevent bullying in our school?*), local community (*How can we educate our community about the impact that individuals' decisions have on others?*), national (*Can we create a short film that will change politician's attitudes to climate change?*) or global (*How can poetry be used to inspire people to donate money to combat the global food crisis?*). The best problems, of course, are those identified by students through their own personal experience or through their own in-depth inquiry. To help students with their problem-finding, you could use this sentence from the AC as stimulus for discussion and brainstorming: *Complex issues require responses that take account of ethical considerations such as human rights and responsibilities, animal rights, environmental issues and global justice.* It simply is NOT enough to have our students writing persuasive speeches, research articles or poems about these issues, handing them in to their teacher for a mark and ticking a box. We MUST empower our young people to actually actively take part in making a contribution to their world – to truly contribute their ideas to solving complex problems. This means ensuring that their learning has a public audience.

Of course, we can't expect one class doing PBL to solve the world's problems – but many hands make light work. According to the AC, '*technologies bring local and distant communities into classrooms, exposing students to knowledge and global concerns as never before.* With the capacity to bring others into our classroom via Skype, Edmodo, social media etc., we have the capacity to work together toward incremental changes to our problematic world. Giving students a taste of what their own personal capacity is, and to develop their understanding of themselves as ethical human beings, is really central to our jobs as teachers.

INTER-CULTURAL UNDERSTANDING

For the AC, inter-cultural understanding '*assists young people to become responsible local and global citizens, equipped through their education for living and working together in an interconnected world*'.

Creating learning experiences that provide students with the opportunity to connect and collaborate with students from backgrounds different from their own truly does nurture inter-cultural understanding. During PBL, students develop essential 21st-century skills as they establish connections with other schools or with experts from outside of school. PBL provides the students with '*the ability to relate to and communicate across cultures at local, regional and global levels*'.

Using this approach to learning truly opens our eyes, as teachers, to the potential connections our young people can make with others. It doesn't have to be connections from outside of the school either, as inter-cultural connections within schools are just as worthwhile.

It is essential that we continue to value our young people as the future of our world and support them as best we can to develop or strengthen these important attributes of good humans. We truly do feel that an approach to learning such as PBL that is experiential, authentic and engaging, provides our learners with the BEST opportunity to hone these very important values and attributes.

HOW DOES PBL RUN IN THE ENGLISH CLASSROOM?

There are five key components that we include in every project to ensure successful student engagement and deep learning. *These are a driving question, a project outline, an expert, a hook lesson and a project wall.* These elements will help you to structure each project and to keep students focused on their learning goals.

DRIVING QUESTION

This term was developed by the Buck Institute for Education (BIE, 2014) and is fundamental to every project. A driving question is an open-ended question forming the basis for the inquiry that takes place throughout the project.

As PBL is fundamentally an inquiry-based approach to teaching and learning, the driving question is the motivating force behind every project. It is the basis of all inquiry throughout the project, 'driving' all of what students will 'need to know' and do along the way.

A driving question is like the foundations of a building or the launchpad for a space mission. Everything starts from there. Driving questions also provide focus for learners: What are we trying to learn? How do we go about answering the question? What do we need to know, make and do? How do we demonstrate our learning?

Driving questions should be open ended, not something that can be answered simply by picking up an encyclopaedia, textbook or by an Internet search. This ensures that students will need to engage in extended inquiry in order to complete the project. It is often helpful to embed the content focus and final product within the driving question in order to help students understand what they are heading toward as they progress through the project. Wherever possible, educators should consider how to leave the product open to student choice and personal preference, and therefore ownership over the product that eventually comes to light. It is also a good idea to include the audience for whom learners will be creating within the driving question. Some examples of open-ended questions, both tried and tested, and hypothetical questions are listed below, with content, target audience and product explained. They are not driving questions for specifically 'English' projects, rather multi-disciplinary projects.

EXAMPLE ONE: *How can we wow Wagga with our writing?*

For this project the syllabus content is imaginative writing, the product could be any range of texts, and the target audience is a class of students from Wagga Wagga, New South Wales, as well as the local library.

EXAMPLE TWO: *What's the best design for a dragon trap?*

This is a driving question that we have used successfully at professional development events. In these cases the 'public audience' was ourselves, posing as dragon keepers. However if you were to use this question with, for instance, a high-school English class, the public audience could just as feasibly be a local wildlife trapper or someone who works for the dog pound. The syllabus content would be persuasive writing, as students would need to pitch their final designs, also linked to science/technology and creative arts.

EXAMPLE THREE: *Which Australian animal deserves our protection?*

For this project, students need to research Australian animals to learn about their features, behaviours and habitats. Students would need to then create an informative text explaining the animals and why they think their chosen creature is most deserving of conservation efforts. The public audience could be a class of students from another country who would also learn about their local animals to create a text for the Australian class.

PROJECT OUTLINE

A project outline is a document explaining the rationale and aims, audience, products and learning intentions of each project. These can be handed out to students to be put into their project packets (explained later), laminated and posted on to the classroom project wall (explained later), or both. If you have access to laptops, PCs or tablets, you might like to create a digital project outline using Google Docs, Weebly or Canvas.

Project outlines provide students with an idea of what they will be learning, the products they will be making and for what audience, and the steps they need to be taking along the way in order to successfully complete the project. Project outlines serve a dual purpose – they help students with project management and understanding learning expectations, and they are also great for the teacher as a formative assessment tool. The 'discover, create, share' structure enables the process of the project to be broken down into manageable steps so each student or team of students' progress can be tracked at every stage.

An effective project outline should do the following things.

- **Be visually appealing.** No one wants to be given a boring document that basically explains what will be happening in class along with all of the work that needs to be done in order to pass the required assessments. Visually appealing project outlines are more likely to get students wanting to engage with what they're doing, plus they look great on your classroom project wall.
- **Clearly display the driving question.** The driving question is one of the main motivators behind any good project. By having it clearly displayed on the project outline, the class can constantly refer back to it and assess how they are progressing along the way to answering it. There are usually a number of related questions, guided by the 'need to knows' of the project, and it is quite useful to include these on the outline to help guide students along the way.
- **Clearly outline the process, products and audience of the project.** Projects can usually be broken down into three distinct phases: An initial inquiry, or 'discover' phase in which students engage in extensive research around a particular topic; an additional production stage in which students 'create' some sort of product for their intended audience; and a final stage in which they prepare to present or 'share' their product with the audience.

EXPERT/ROCK STAR

This step is probably one of the most daunting in PBL. It requires you to reach out to a complete stranger and ask them to do you a favour – and, most often, free of charge. We use the term 'rock star' to refer to people who have been invited to participate in a project in the role of 'expert' or 'audience'. This term was coined by the Buck Institute for Education in their fantastic YouTube video, 'Project Based Learning: Explained' at *www.youtube.com/watch?v=LMCZvGesRz8*. It is always great if someone can fill both of these roles – coming in early to support students' initial inquiry, and then returning later to provide students with feedback (and praise) on their final product and/or presentation. Throughout the sample projects you will find suggestions on how to be successful at finding your rock star. Remember that energetic, fun and engaging invitations (from students or from you) are more likely to have a positive response.

HOOK LESSONS

The hook lesson might just be the most fun part of any project. The hook lesson comes at the very beginning of a project or entry event. It is sometimes referred to as the project launch. The idea of a hook lesson is to hook your students' interest in a particular idea, form, problem or text. It also aims to initiate inquiry. A hook might be the length of your regular English lesson, or it might be a whole-day or half-day event or excursion. A hook lesson should be high-energy, fun, challenging and engaging enough to get your students starting to ask questions about the project and interested enough to want to learn more.

When planning your hook lesson, you need to think about what you believe your students will find the most interesting about your project – like modern adaptations of literary classics or how far a grenade could be thrown in the First World War. You might think about making connections between the themes in a text and contemporary life – shaming those with bad fashion sense or the way that rap music continues to rail against discrimination. Now, think about fun ways of hooking students into thinking about these ideas. Students often enjoy games or competing in teams – how could you make the key content and skills of your project obvious through a fun game of trivia?

Each of the sample projects in this book include examples of hook lessons that you may choose to use, or adapt to use, with your class.

PROJECT WALLS

A project wall is a wall inside the classroom dedicated to the learning that takes place throughout the course of the project. It is a good idea to place the project outline on the project wall, along with the 'need to knows', any rubrics that are being used, and of course lots of examples of student work to display and celebrate their learning. Project walls typically start out quite bare and become increasingly vibrant, bright and colourful throughout the course of the project. By the end, it's quite common to have run out of space on your wall. As with project outlines, if you're in a school that has easy access to a lot of technology you might want to create a digital project wall. We've found that tools like Weebly and Glogster are great for this, but there are many other options as well. This will also be a great option for teachers who don't have access to the same classroom every day.

Project walls are a terrific, engaging way for both teachers and students to track their learning throughout the course of the project. Having the driving question and need to knows posted on the classroom wall ensures that they are constantly referred back to in order to formatively assess which aspects of the inquiry process have been completed and what else still needs to be learned. Student work can be showcased on the project wall along with any language features learned throughout the course of the project. This is useful not only for the project currently being undertaken but also for any future projects and any other classroom activities in which these language features might be revised or of use.

Project walls are also a great way to celebrate success. As they typically grow throughout the project, it's a great way to look back on how far the class has come and to reflect on the learning. Remember, project walls are about tracking learning, so don't feel the need to only put perfect completed work on there. Celebrate learning by posting up peer-feedback and student drafts. An additional advantage of the project wall is that it brightens up the classroom. We love it when visitors come to our classrooms and see our project walls. It's quite common for them to take pictures of the learning being celebrated on my classroom walls.

There's no exact method for making a project wall. Typically all you need is a blank wall in your classroom. From here you put up your project outline with the driving question and need to knows. You then begin to add student work as the class progresses through the project. This would include any language features that the class has been learning, aspects of creative writing or narrative components such as setting, plot and character development, as well as things such as storyboards, artworks and photos of classroom activities. If you use things like KWL tables or teamwork rubrics, these can also be placed on the project wall for reference. Project walls are fantastic for revision and reflection.

Example project walls

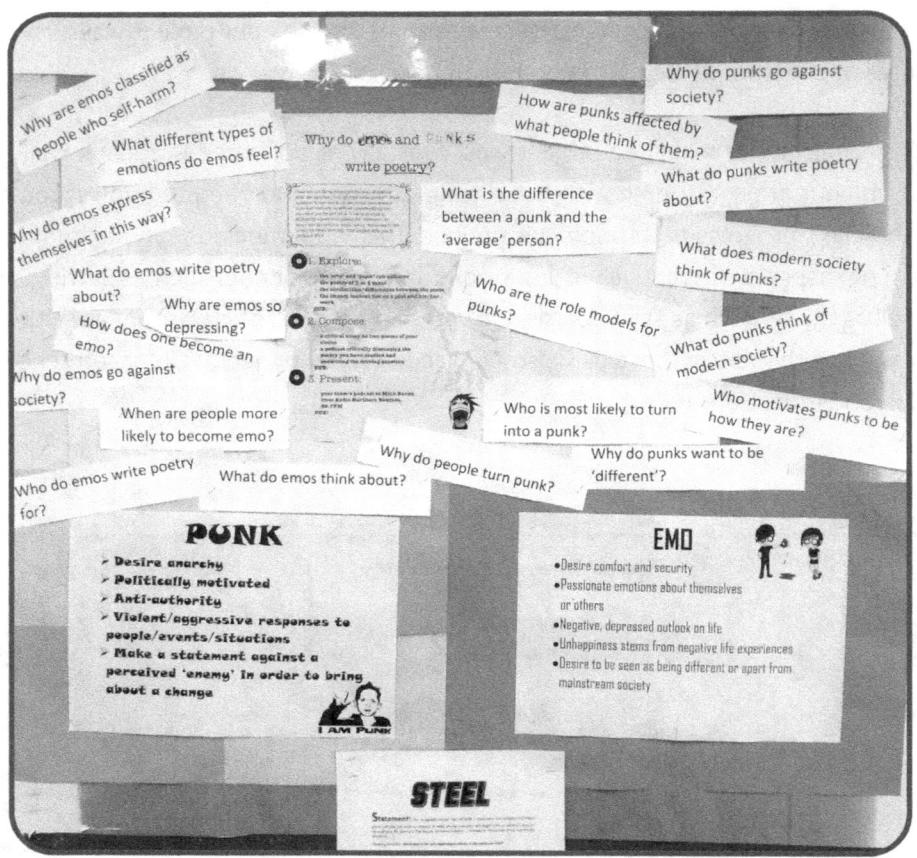

A WORD ABOUT PBL AND ASSESSMENT

Assessment is an integral part of Project Based Learning. It sees learning as an ongoing process, and as a result champions the use of formative-assessment strategies that help students identify learning goals and strategies to achieve them. Our three-stage approach to PBL has been designed with assessment in mind. Student learning is assessed at each of the stages using a range of strategies. For each sample project, we have included suggested strategies for assessment at each of these three stages of learning. Our preference is that marks and grades are not given for project work (see explanation below), however how you choose to formally assess your students will be dependent on your school's assessment policy and your own personal beliefs.

Our approach to PBL is all about the process. It makes it slower, messier and sometimes 'look' less successful than those cool videos you see of successful PBL projects on YouTube. But this is okay with us because our focus is learning and the process is the learning. One of the most effective types of assessment is peer assessment. The scariest thing for teachers when implementing peer assessment is the time that it takes to 'perfect'. Students simply don't have the skill set to effectively assess the work of themselves or their peers. They need to be taught how to do this – they need support and modelling. They need to be fully involved in the process, but most of all they need to be given time. Time? It's the one thing most teachers feel they don't have enough of, but we have to let go of our focus on content and reclaim the higher ground and TEACH SKILLS. Luckily for us English teachers we have this built directly into the Australian Curriculum: English.

We were influenced in the design of our scaffolds for peer and self-assessment by the work of Geoff Petty. We think he's great because he has so many wonderful resources for free online. Type his name into Google and you will find them. Petty argues that too much of the feedback we give students is BACKWARD looking and often this feedback is quantitative (numerical e.g. 7/10; 70%) but even qualitative feedback (words e.g. 'You didn't begin your sentences with a capital letter') more often than not looks backwards at what WAS done or, typically, WASN'T done. Petty advocates for a method of feedback that is both backwards and forwards looking … and to do that he uses the 'goals, medals and missions' protocol, which you will have noticed on the checklists we've included in each project. It's really neat because the language is accessible to all age groups and it is non-threatening. Essentially the 'goals' are the criteria for the product (be it a short film, an essay or a presentation) and the 'medals' are what has been achieved (this is the backward-looking stuff) and always takes the form of positive statements, e.g. 'Your introduction is strong.' The 'missions' are the important part of the protocol – this is 'feed-forward' as it is looking at what the student needs to work on to improve the product or the next product.

When introducing the idea of 'feedback' and 'feed-forward' to students, it will probably take a little while for them to understand it. Try using a real-world example. Say you're five years old and your dad and teenage brother take you to the park to teach you how to ride your bike without training wheels. Your dad gives you a push, you pedal for a bit and then fall into a bush. Your brother calls out, 'Er, you loser! You fell into the bush!' and your dad stands there holding up a sign with the number 3 on it. That is all the feedback you receive – one is qualitative and one is quantitative. What is your response? You kick your bike and you storm off. No more bike-riding for you, it's too hard and you're terrible at it – the feedback of your loved-ones told you so. But what if the imaginary dad did something different? What if he gave a medal for what the child did (the feedback), saying something like, 'You managed to stay upright for two metres'? What if he then gave his child a mission (feed-forward), saying something like, 'Next time I want you to pedal a bit faster and I want you to keep your weight in the middle and avoid leaning to the right'? Sounds like what every dad would do, right? This is 'real-world' feedback, but it's not always classroom-world feedback. I'm sure your students will understand that analogy.

To our students, we try to avoid the words 'peer assessment'. We prefer 'peer feedback'. The word assessment is scary and doesn't reflect the learning that is inherent in this process, rather it focuses more on judgement. A good tip is to get your students to develop the criteria for a product or presentation with you. Write learning goals up on the board, negotiate how to express them and then add them to the checklist proforma given in the following section. We suggest that you phrase the criteria as questions and avoid using the word 'student' if possible, as it's preferable to refer to students as writers, essayists, reviewers, filmmakers etc. This distances the students from feeling like it is a personal criticism being given. What we've discovered is that students need to provide evidence for their feedback – if they only have to tick boxes, they can easily do this randomly and without thought. If you look at the next example, you'll see that each point in the criteria (the 'goals') has a number beside it. This number is a kind of 'code' that students use to annotate the work being 'assessed'. We encourage students to add a cross or tick beside the number so the writer can identify if they have or haven't met that criteria in a specific place. We tell students that they must resist writing corrections on the work (such as spelling and punctuation), as we want to encourage thoughtful revision and independence. We don't want students that need teachers to rewrite their work for them. Students are also required to give written feedback in the form of medals and missions – these must be written in sentences and use the language of the criteria. We have had a lot of success with this approach to assessment, and we hope you will too.

Often the assessment we have in our schools doesn't actually assess the real learning gains students make. Too often assessment is summative, assessing the end product of learning and not the process. We believe this is problematic. The biggest problem with summative assessment is that it does not give students the feedback they need to improve. If students fail to be provided with opportunities for teacher, peer and self-feedback throughout the learning cycle, students easily become disengaged and demotivated, and continue to make the same errors unchecked. Of course another problem of summative assessment is the failure to assess those skills that have been dubbed '21st-century skills', or as we prefer to call them the 'skills for life beyond school'. These skills include cooperation, critical and creative thinking, and the ability to use digital technologies to enhance learning, collaboration, presentation skills, problem-solving, confidence, ethical thinking and persistence. All of these things are so essential to being a thriving, successful individual today. These things have not been officially assessed as long as I have been teaching. As you can see in Part Three, we believe assessing these skills is important to support student learning.

Built into quality PBL is a series of investigations, products and a final presentation of learning. Each task involves teacher, self and peer-feedback. Students actively engage in goal-setting and reflection tasks. This is authentic learning. Assessment is a massive driver of teaching and learning – we can't ignore it.

PART TWO
SAMPLE PROJECTS

YEAR 9:

1. MAD BLOOD
2. MOBILE LEARNING
3. SPEAK UP
4. TEENS UNITE
5. MIDNIGHT SNACKS

YEAR 10:

1. EMOTIONAL EXCESS
2. MORE THAN MEETS THE EYE
3. SOMETHING WICKED
4. WILD AT HEART
5. ENGLISH COMPOSITION PROJECT (ECP)

YEAR 9

1. MAD BLOOD

PROJECT AT A GLANCE:

 **DRIVING QUESTION:** What can we learn from tragedy?

 DISCOVER: Students read and view Shakespeare's *Romeo and Juliet*, analyse language, structure and narrative and research connections between the play and their world.

 CREATE: Students individually write a personal essay answering the driving question, and in a team perform a scene from the play.

 SHARE: The collected class essays will be published online using Booksie OR a hard-copy anthology published using Blurb. Each team will perform their scene from the play for an audience including family/friends/invited guests or another year group.

TAKE IT FURTHER: Film the performances and post them to the faculty/school YouTube channel and share it with another class studying *Romeo and Juliet*.

 ASSESSMENT: Students will be assessed individually for their personal essay and as a group for their performance.

 21ST-CENTURY SKILLS: collaboration and creative thinking.

LITERACY: Grammar – active/passive voice, topic sentences, clauses; Spelling – words with Latin and Greek roots; Reading – monitoring and making connections

MODE: Writing (personal essay) and representing (performance)

TYPE OF TEXT: Persuasive (personal essay) and imaginative texts (play/performance)

LANGUAGE FEATURES OF TEXTS: iambic pentameter, blank verse, soliloquy, aside, embedded stage directions, apostrophe, allusions, oxymoron

POSSIBLE TEXTS: *Romeo and Juliet* by William Shakespeare; *No Fear Shakespeare: Romeo and Juliet*; graphic novel version of *Romeo and Juliet*; Franco Zeffirelli's *Romeo and Juliet*; Baz Luhrmann's *Romeo and Juliet*.

What can *Romeo and Juliet* teach me about conflict that I can't learn from **C.O.D.** or **The Voice**?

🔍 Investigate & Discover

1. Investigate the nature of conflict
2. Discover the plot, characters, style and themes of *Romeo and Juliet*.

📜 Rehearse & Compose

1. In a small team you will select and rehearse one scene from *Romeo and Juliet* that illustrates a 'lesson' worth learning about conflict.
2. Compose a personal essay answering the project's DQ using supporting evidence from *Romeo and Juliet*.

🎤 Perform & Publish

1. Perform your selected scene in front of your peers and explain what we can learn from the conflict presented in *Romeo and Juliet*.
2. Publish your essay in a class anthology of essays on *Romeo and Juliet* to be made available in the school library.

REPRODUCIBLE — PART TWO: SAMPLE PROJECTS YEAR 9 — 1. MAD BLOOD

What can we Learn from Tragedy?

Inquire

1. Complete a KWL table about this project.
2. Read Shakespeare's *Romeo and Juliet* to develop a critical understanding of:
   - Shakespeare's language and theatre
   - the play's plot, characters, style and issues raised

Produce

1. In a small team you will select one scene from *Romeo and Juliet* that illustrates a 'lesson' worth learning about tragedy.
2. Write a personal essay answering the project's DQ with supporting evidence from *Romeo and Juliet*.

Present

1. Perform your selected scene in front of your peers and explain what we can learn from the tragedy of *Romeo and Juliet*.
2. Submit your polished personal essay to be published in a relevant source. Publish your essay in a class anthology of essays on *Romeo and Juliet* to be made available in the library.

REPRODUCIBLE – PART TWO: SAMPLE PROJECTS YEAR 9 – 1. MAD BLOOD

BEFORE YOU BEGIN

CONTACT EXPERTS/ROCK STARS

This project requires your students to perform scenes from *Romeo and Juliet* in front of an audience. You may choose to give your students a choice about who they would prefer to be in the audience, or you might find it more effective to specify the audience for them. If you choose to specify the audience and include guests from outside of the school, you will likely need to organise invitations to go out quite early in the project, if not before the project begins. Possible guests include actors from a local amateur theatre group, academics who specialise in Shakespeare or the theatre reviewer from the local newspaper.

This project also requires students to write a personal essay responding to the ideas in the play. In order to make this part of the project engaging, you might wish to invite in an expert to speak about persuasive writing, developing an argument or contemporary responses to Shakespeare. Academics or bloggers would be an excellent choice for this role.

MODIFY PROJECT OUTLINE

Look at the two sample project outlines given. They are very similar, however one makes more of an effort to connect to the contemporary textual experiences of Year 9 students. You will need to take some time to decide which project outline you think is most suitable for your students. Remember that PBL is all about engaging students through making content significant for their needs and interests. You will also need to modify the project outline to indicate due dates for formative and summative assessment.

ORGANISE PROJECT PACKETS

This is an important organisation strategy that we use a lot in PBL. For this project, students will be working in small teams. A project packet is essentially a small folder or document wallet given to each team that contains all of the essential materials for students to be successful with the project. These remain in the classroom and are accessed by students each lesson. Of course, there are so many technology options available that mean that your project packets do not need to be paper based. The benefits of having digital project packets and ePortfolios means that students can add to and access them when they're at home, and so can you. Some of the online tools that would be great for this application include: Google Docs, Blackboard, Edmodo, Glogster, Weebly, Evernote and Canvas.

PLAN PROJECT TEAMS

Planning teams is inherently difficult, as you must consider the personality as well as the skill level of each student in your class. For this project, it is best to select a mixed team, taking into consideration the following skills: performance, public speaking, communication and creativity. Try to balance the teams to ensure that you have even numbers of outgoing and reserved students. Performing in front of an audience is daunting for many students, add to this a Shakespearean text and students are going to need to feel very supported and comfortable. As such, try to ensure each student has at least one person they trust and are on friendly terms with in their team.

CREATE SPACE FOR A PROJECT WALL

This project wall will need to be updated regularly so students can see their understanding of the play grow. Start your project wall with the title of the project 'Mad Blood' – this is a phrase from the play, so try to encourage your students to keep their eyes out to discover who says it. In equally large writing, put up your project's driving question – students need to see this as it will drive them through the project and inspire them to think critically. You will also need an A3 colour printout of the project outline. Leave space for a project calendar (or put up a blank one and have a student fill it in as you negotiate due dates etc.), the 'need to know' list of questions and a good amount of space for 'key terms'. Since this is a project exploring a Shakespearean play, it won't take long to identify new words and terms that students previously did not know. Remember that these need to be blank at the beginning of the project, as this information will be added by students during the 'discover' stage of learning. Use as much colour as you can, because it is important that students are attracted to it, as it is a visible record of their learning. You might even like to nominate a student to be responsible for adding new information to the 'key terms' or 'need to know' spaces. If you don't happen to have your own classroom, and therefore you can't add information to a wall, how about creating a digital project wall? Online tools like Glogster, Weebly and Canvas are great for this purpose.

LAUNCH YOUR PROJECT

HOOK LESSON

There are so many possibilities for how to hook your students' interest in this project. The first thing to consider is what the main conceptual focus of the project is; in this instance it could be either tragedy or conflict as per the sample project outlines. You might choose to look at other concepts like obedience, gender or love. Another approach may focus on Shakespeare as the most important element of the project. Finally, you might decide to focus on the type of product to be created, in this instance a personal essay and drama performance. Some hook lessons based on these approaches might be:

- a mini drama activity where students are asked to identify a type of conflict or tragedy (e.g. conflict with parents or broken mobile phone) and put it on a Post-It note. Students are given, at random, one of these Post-Its. They are put into teams of three and each team must select one conflict/tragedy to perform for the class. The class must try to guess the type of conflict/tragedy and one team will win 'best performance' at the end.
- a Shakespearean insults duel using one of the many great mobile apps
- watching excerpts from *Shakespeare in Love*
- mini debates on topics such as 'video games teach us nothing' and 'reality television kills your brain'
- a game of trivia where students answer questions about video games, reality television and Shakespeare.

POSE DRIVING QUESTION

The lesson after the 'hook lesson' is very, very important. This is the lesson where students are given access to the project's driving question for the first time. This project's driving question is: What can we learn from tragedy?

Of course, if you'd like to use the other sample project outline, then your project's driving question will be: What can *Romeo and Juliet* teach me about conflict that I can't learn from C.O.D or The Voice? Of course, it's also a great activity to get students to design the project's driving question with you. This can be done through a class discussion. We have done this a number of times with our classes and it is always surprising what students come up with. When they have ownership over part of the project design, they feel ownership of their learning.

Once you pose this question to the students (we often put it up on the whiteboard or the interactive whiteboard), get each individual to immediately write down their own, un-mediated personal response to it. This will become their 'hypothesis', which will be tested and reshaped as they work through the 'discover' learning stage.

HAND OUT PROJECT OUTLINE

We recommend that the project outline is printed off in colour or printed onto coloured paper. This sets it apart from other pieces of paper that students will receive or use during the project. The project outline is a very important document as it acts as a flyer for learning. As soon as you hand the project outline out, have students sit quietly and read through it, using a pen or highlighter to identify any information that they feel they do not understand or that they have questions about. This is an essential step, as this information becomes part of what the class has identified as what they 'need to know'. It is a good idea to encourage students to keep this project outline in their team's project packet or their own personal portfolio. We have had great success with students keeping a personal plastic sleeve folder as their 'learning portfolio'. If you have access to mobile devices like tablets or laptops, or a bank of PCs, you might consider having students create digital portfolios using Google Docs. They will use this for the entire year of projects.

ESTABLISH NEED TO KNOW

This is such an integral part of PBL. PBL is about inquiry that is led by the students. One of the best ways to begin inquiry is to ask questions. Once students have considered the driving question and have read through the project outline, they will no doubt begin to ask a lot of questions. This is a good thing. Your job is to not answer the questions, but rather to encourage students to record and develop their questions further. You may like to do this as a class group — having students call out their questions and allocating one student the role of scribe. These questions can then be recorded onto the project wall, becoming a guide for students' learning through the project. If you think students need to develop their questioning strategies, you could try using the star-bursting technique. Have students draw a six-pointed star in the middle of a sheet of paper. On each point write: where, what, how, when, why, who. Encourage students to think of as many questions about the project (and its related content) beginning with each word, and record them on their paper. You will be surprised by the richness and diversity of the questions students ask. This lesson also provides an opportunity for students to begin thinking about the audience for their presentation and product. For example: Who will it be? What are their interests? How do we cater for these? Note that all of these questions will stem from the original driving question, and this means that you must have a strong driving question that has the potential to generate further questions and set the stage for students' inquiry. Below is an example.

SET UP TEAMS

This is a fairly quick step in PBL, but it can be very painful for students. Most students will initially resent being 'forced' to work with peers that they don't usually associate with. This is normal. Our experience is that after the first few projects, students become much more accustomed to working with a range of peers, and even begin to acknowledge the strengths of others with whom they may not usually work. As a teacher, you need to think about what the benefits will be to having students working in teams for a specific project. The obvious reason is that we want to develop teamwork skills such as collaboration, communication and collective decision-making, however other valid reasons include appreciating diversity in learning styles and deepening understanding by considering a range of perspectives on an issue. When teams are first established, it is a good idea to encourage them to choose a team name – this gives them a collective identity. Try to remember the team names and refer to each team by their name at some point during each lesson. We find it handy to run a team-building activity such as devising a team contract where, as a team, they commit to certain expected behaviours such as being on time to class, not interrupting when someone else is talking or putting in their personal best each lesson. You might like to provide your students with a scaffold for this, and we've provided you with an example in the 'Part Three: Additional Resources' section of this book. Routine is very important to PBL, so encourage students to select someone in the team to be responsible for collecting the team's project packet each lesson and someone else to be the team spokesperson for when they need to share ideas with the teacher or class.

CREATE A PROJECT CALENDAR

A project calendar is designed to keep students forward-focused. PBL is a student-directed methodology, where students are required to take responsibility for their own learning. As such, a project calendar can help students keep themselves organised and ensure that they are working toward clearly established deadlines. These deadlines should be negotiated with the teacher as a whole class, however there will be times when individual teams will have different deadlines to ensure that learning is differentiated effectively. We recommend that a project calendar includes clearly identified dates for formative assessment — that is, assessment of learning through strategies like plans, drafts, mini-presentations, quizzes and meetings with team leaders. This project has students completing two products — a personal essay and a performance. The project calendar must reflect opportunities for teams to receive feedback on these products at the process stage. Students will also negotiate with the teacher opportunities for direct instruction — this is where the teacher runs a traditional, teacher-centred lesson — and time to receive and apply feedback. For this project, students are required to engage with a Shakespearean play, and therefore a number of lessons will need to be dedicated to whole-class instruction while the play is read and some scenes performed. See the calendar on the next page.

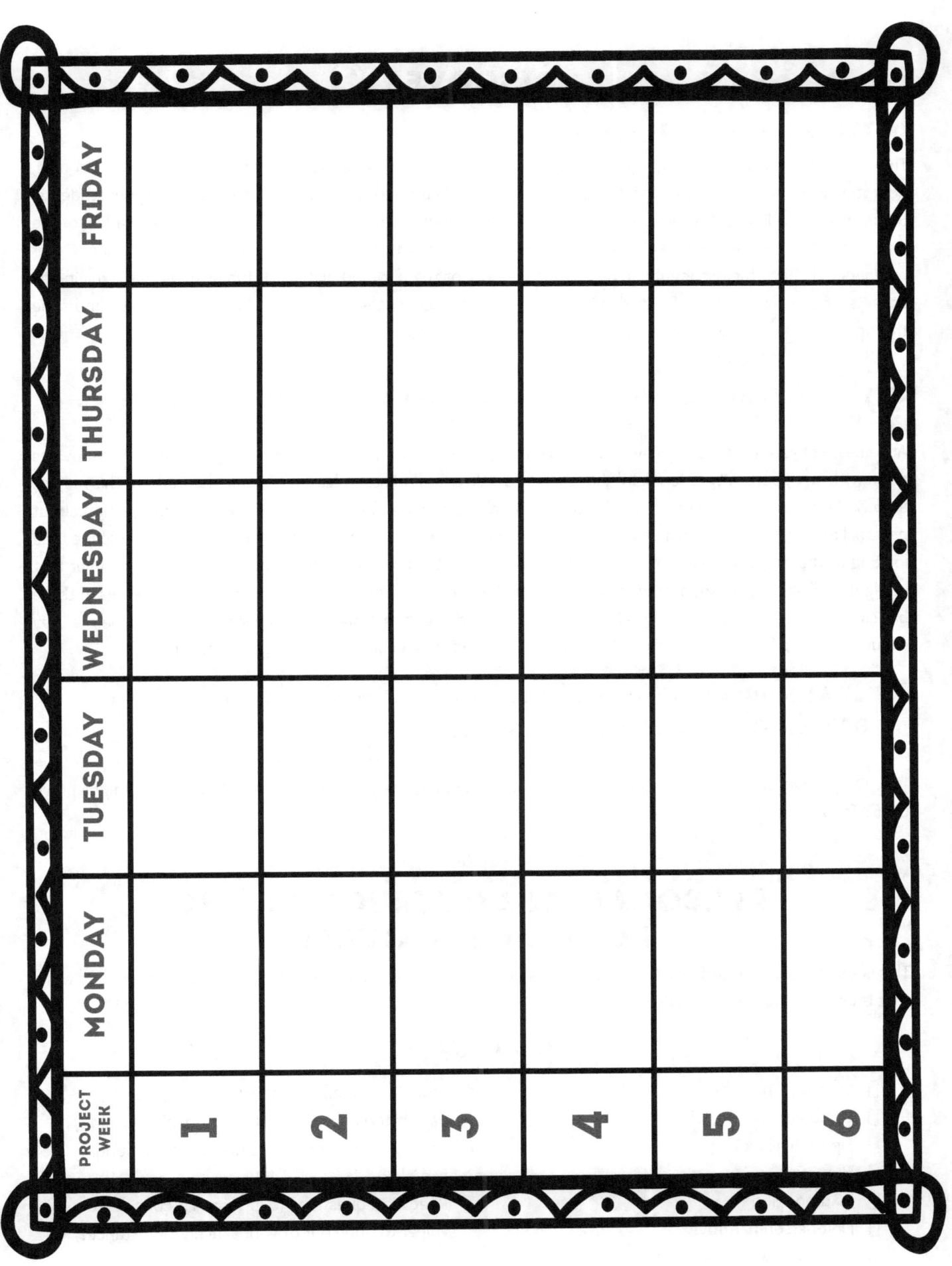

REPRODUCIBLE – PART TWO: SAMPLE PROJECTS YEAR 9 – 1. MAD BLOOD

DISCOVER

GETTING TO KNOW THE PLAY

This project has an extended 'inquiry' phase because students must engage with a Shakespearean text. Of course, how you decide to get your students to engage with the texts is up to you and highly dependent on your students. Some teachers will want their students to engage with the written text through a whole-class close reading of the play. Some teachers will read extracts of the play but spend most of the time watching a film adaptation. Other teachers may have their students engage with the story of the play and watch YouTube videos that explain key aspects of the play. Ultimately, students are required to discover the play's plot, characters, themes and style through a process of inquiry, whether that is guided or independent.

GETTING TO KNOW THE STRUCTURE AND LANGUAGE OF A PERSONAL ESSAY

At some point your students will have identified that they 'need to know' how to write a personal essay. This provides them with an opportunity to 'book in' the teacher to deliver a whole-class lesson of some description. This may be a lively class discussion, a series of collaborative activities or providing students with written information about personal essays. When supporting students with their discovery of a new type of text, it is important to spend time looking at the language features specific to this type of text, as well as spelling, punctuation and grammar that students will likely need support with. While it is highly likely that you will identify common weaknesses in these basics when you're reading initial drafts, it is still a good idea to 'front-load' by addressing likely errors before they occur. Below is a list of basic skills that you might want to focus on before students begin to write.

GRAMMAR: active/passive voice, topic sentences, clauses and clause combinations
SPELLING: words with Latin and Greek roots

On the next two pages is a brief overview of the language features of a personal essay that might prove useful for your students.

PERSONAL ESSAY: STRUCTURE AND LANGUAGE FEATURES

This is a summary that outlines the main features of the personal essay. If you don't know the meaning of a word that is used on this page, Google it.

LANGUAGE FEATURES

- ☐ Emotive language
- ☐ Symbolism
- ☐ Figurative language
- ☐ Humour
- ☐ Juxtaposition
- ☐ First-person narrative
- ☐ Personal, subjective voice
- ☐ Modal verbs (e.g. must/will), nouns (e.g. possibility) and adverbs (e.g. probably, certainly)
- ☐ Variety of sentence types (simple, compound, complex)
- ☐ Rhetorical questions (e.g. Why is it considered vulgar to drink out of your saucer, for instance?)

STRUCTURE

INTRODUCTION may outline the topic or main ideas of the essay, but it may also just hint at these.

'Before the swallow, before the daffodil, and not much later than the snowdrop, the common toad salutes the coming of spring after his own fashion, which is to emerge from a hole in the ground, where he has lain buried since the previous autumn, and crawl as rapidly as possible towards the nearest suitable patch of water. Something — some kind of shudder in the earth, or perhaps merely a rise of a few degrees in the temperature — has told him that it is time to wake up: though a few toads appear to sleep the clock round and miss out a year from time to time — at any rate, I have more than once dug them up, alive and apparently well, in the middle of the summer.'

BODY PARAGRAPHS can be rambling and unfocused, but sometimes they are very tightly structured and make a concise, logical argument.

'I mention the spawning of the toads because it is one of the phenomena of spring which most deeply appeal to me, and because the toad, unlike the skylark and the primrose, has never had much of a boost from poets. But I am aware that many people do not like reptiles or amphibians, and I am not suggesting that in order to enjoy the spring you have to take an interest in toads. There are also the crocus, the missel-thrush, the cuckoo, the blackthorn, etc. The point is that the pleasures of spring are available to everybody, and cost nothing. Even in the most sordid street the coming of spring will register itself by some sign or other, if it is only a brighter blue between the chimney pots or the vivid green of an elder sprouting on a blitzed site. Indeed it is remarkable how Nature goes on existing unofficially, as it were, in the very heart of London.'

CONCLUSION nearly always leaves the reader wanting to continue reading, or to start asking questions of the writer.

'At any rate, spring is here, even in London N1, and they can't stop you enjoying it. This is a satisfying reflection. How many a time have I stood watching the toads mating, or a pair of hares having a boxing match in the young corn, and thought of all the important persons who would stop me enjoying this if they could. But luckily they can't. So long as you are not actually ill, hungry, frightened or immured in a prison or a holiday camp, spring is still spring. The atom bombs are piling up in the factories, the police are prowling through the cities, the lies are streaming from the loudspeakers, but the earth is still going round the sun, and neither the dictators nor the bureaucrats, deeply as they disapprove of the process, are able to prevent it.'

(All quotations on this page are from *Some Thoughts on the Common Toad* by George Orwell, in the public domain in Australia and accessible here: *https://ebooks.adelaide.edu.au/o/orwell/george/o79e/part45.html*)

FORMATIVE ASSESSMENT

During this inquiry, it is essential that you take frequent opportunities to check for understanding. There are many formative assessment strategies that can be used to check for understanding, however some are more suited to this project than others. The following formative assessment strategies should be used during the inquiry stage of the project to help you assess students' understanding:

- multiple-choice quiz on the play's characters, plot and themes
- team mini presentation focusing on one aspect of the play (characters, plot and themes)
- exit slips asking students to summarise the scenes from *Romeo and Juliet* read in class that lesson
- matching activity where students match a personal essay language feature with its definition
- give each team one or two of the 'need to know' questions from the project wall and have them try to answer them with the class.

If you discover that there is a gap in students' knowledge or understanding, then take the time to address this as well as you can. If it is a problem shared by the class, address it as a whole class. If it is a problem shared by a few students, bring them together in a small team and chat with them about ways to address the issue. This can be done while the rest of the class is working on an activity individually or in their project teams.

CREATE

This part of the project should take approximately half of the time allocated. Students will spend time planning and drafting their personal essay. The handout on the next page will help students with planning their essays. Once each student has written a draft, time should be given for peer feedback using the peer-feedback checklist. Once students have given and received peer feedback, students should spend some time refining their essays based on the suggestions of their peers, and their teacher if time permits. Final personal essays can be posted online to share with a wider audience or published in an anthology and printed using an online book publisher like Blurb.

Now that students have a solid appreciation of the play, they will begin working in teams on their drama performance. It is a good idea to try to find a space larger than the classroom, such as the drama room, school hall or the school oval. This will give students the freedom to experiment with their performances without feeling shy or embarrassed. On the following pages there is a brief handout that will support your students through the selection and rehearsal of their scene. Formative assessment continues throughout this process, as you now have the opportunity to spend time with each team and help with their performance. You might like to use the 'Performance Checklist' to give students formative feedback at this stage.

WHAT ARE SOME THINGS I SHOULD TALK ABOUT IN MY PERSONAL ESSAY?

1. Make sure your essay answers the driving question: *What can we learn from tragedy?*

   This is a personal essay – this means you get to write about your own thoughts, opinions and experiences on the issue. The issue that you need to focus on is tragedy. Discuss your thoughts with your team members to see what they believe we can learn from the tragedy of *Romeo and Juliet*.

   Now you need to ask yourself whether these 'lessons' are appropriate to other tragedies, such as man-made tragedies like 9/11 or natural tragedies like floods. Or what about everyday tragedy like the loss of a family member to cancer or having your house burgled? Do we learn different things from these experiences?

2. You might want to think about the role that tragedy plays in our lives. It certainly is an unwelcome experience, but does it have its place? If we think about literature (novels, films, plays etc.) then we will see that tragic stories seem to feature a lot. Why do we like to watch tragic events happen to other people? Is there a purpose to experiencing other people's tragedy? Does it help us in some way? Can you think of an example of a film, book or play that you have watched that tells the story of someone else's tragic experience? Why did you watch it? You might like to refer to this in your essay. What about the news that focuses on tragic events? Why do you watch this? Maybe you could include an example of this in your essay.

   Your answers to any or all of the questions in the paragraph above could work well in your personal essay.

3. When you have decided on what you would like to focus on in your personal essay – maybe one thing that we can learn from tragedy, maybe two or three things that we can learn – you should think about identifying a few examples from the play *Romeo and Juliet* that support your ideas. Try to add quotes or descriptions of scenes and the characters involved when you're talking about the play.

4. Your personal essay should feature the introduction, body, conclusion structure BUT your paragraphs can be quite loosely structured. Make sure each idea expressed in your paragraphs is supported with an example – this could be from *Romeo and Juliet*, from your own experience in life or from another film/book you have read or viewed. You should try to write at least THREE body paragraphs.

5. Focus on making your personal essay engaging – use the language features suggested on the 'Overview of the Personal Essay' handout.

6. Have fun.

WHAT CAN WE LEARN FROM TRAGEDY?

GROUP PERFORMANCE OF A SCENE FROM *ROMEO AND JULIET*

1. In your project team, negotiate which scene from the play you feel BEST communicates an important life lesson to the audience. This lesson can be about anything, because our argument is that tragedy helps us to learn new things about ourselves, others or the world. It's up to you and your team members to decide what it is we learn from *Romeo and Juliet* and choose a scene that best reflects this.

2. Your scene only needs to run for 3–5 minutes. Have a look in your copy of *Romeo and Juliet* to find your scene. You may need to condense your scene (this means make it shorter by cutting out a character or some words). Do you want to speak the Shakespearean lines or the modern English ones? Why?

3. Does everyone have to act? Yes. This means you need to find a scene where there are enough characters OR you swap characters in the middle – you'll have to work out how to do this without ruining the drama.

4. You will need to match actions to the words – you can only do this by getting on your feet and acting it out. Costumes and props are essential elements of drama – bring them and use them well.

5. As a team you need to write one paragraph explaining why you chose your scene and how it helps to answer the driving question, 'What can we learn from tragedy?'

6. REHEARSE, REHEARSE, REHEARSE.

Personal Essay Checklist

	Criteria	Peer Assessment 1			Peer Assessment 2		
		Didn't	Tried	Did	Didn't	Tried	Did
1	Does the essayist establish a personal and distinctive voice throughout the essay?						
2	Are a variety of sentence types used to create pace, mood and focus? Sentence types include simple, compound, complex						
3	Is interesting, varied and appropriate vocabulary used to help the reader better understand the ideas of the personal essay?						
4	Does the essayist answer the driving question by presenting a personal and thoughtful argument?						
5	Does the introduction hint at the ideas in the body and/or directly engage with the driving question?						
6	Are the language features of an essay used to effectively engage readers? Language features may include emotive language, humour, symbolism, figurative language, juxtaposition, first-person narrative, personal, subjective voice and/or modality.						
7	Does the personal essay have correct grammar, punctuation, spelling and paragraphing?						
8	Do body paragraphs present thoughtful and personal ideas that relate to the driving question?						
9	Do body paragraphs provide evidence to support the ideas being discussed in the paragraph?						
10	Does the conclusion of the essay provoke readers' thoughts/emotions/imagination and make them want to continue reading or ask questions of the essayists?						

Main strengths: (medals)

Missions: (Improvements needed for this essay)

REPRODUCIBLE – PART TWO: SAMPLE PROJECTS YEAR 9 – 1. MAD BLOOD

SHARE

You and your students have finally made it to the end of the project. This part of the project will be both stressful and rewarding. Remember that your students are just as anxious at this stage as you are. It is essential that you give your students lots of encouragement and support but don't fall into the trap of doing the work for them. It doesn't matter if their final performance isn't perfect; it simply needs to be a reflection of their learning and effort as a team. At least a week before the final presentation, make sure that you have a good idea about who will be attending and that you have the ideal space for the performance booked. Performance spaces don't need to be formal or fancy, a large flight of outdoor stairs can provide the perfect performance space, or even putting lots of chairs in a big circle on the school oval for a mock Globe Theatre.

SUMMATIVE ASSESSMENT

Remind students that they will be assessed on their performance as a team or as individuals – whichever you choose – and that you will be using a checklist to give them feedback. It is important that students get a copy of the checklist while they are preparing their performance so they understand the success criteria. Enjoy the show.

POST-PROJECT REFLECTION/EVALUATION

Reflection on learning is an integral part of PBL. The best type of reflection is highly defined and focused on the specific learning targets for the project. Ensure your reflection questions allow students to reflect on their development of these skills and capacities. This will allow them to draw a connection between what your goals were, what they did and how they grew as learners. There are so many ways that you can get your students to engage in reflection on their learning. You might get them to record a podcast describing their favourite and least favourite experiences during the project. You could get students to sit together in small groups and share three skills they've mastered and three new facts they've learned. Two students would interview each other and record their reflections for the teacher to read later. We get our students to blog a lot using the 'think, puzzle, explore' method. For this project, get your students to reflect on their experience of this project by answering the questions below. You could have them put their answers in their portfolio to keep as a record of their learning, or they could use one of the other strategies mentioned.

MAD BLOOD – END OF PROJECT REFLECTION

1. One of the learning goals for this project was to be able to support an argument with evidence. How well did you achieve this goal?

2. What did you learn about Shakespeare in this project that you didn't already know?

3. What is one thing about writing a personal essay that you found hard at the beginning of the project, but you find easier now?

4. What are the three most important things you learned during this project?

5. What is something you taught your teacher or classmates during this project?

6. During this project you had to perform in front of an audience. Describe the learning process you took, from choosing your scene to the final performance.

7. What are six adjectives that best describe this project?

YEAR 9
2. MOBILE LEARNING

PROJECT AT A GLANCE

 **DRIVING QUESTION:** How can mobile phones be used to help us learn in high school?

 DISCOVER: Students will research the use of mobile phones in education, focusing on the pros and cons of their use. They will write a report on this information. They will also discover the language forms and features of persuasive texts.

 CREATE: Students will write a speech answering the project's driving question. They will create a PowerPoint slide-show to support their speech.

 SHARE: Students will present their speeches in front of their school principal or head of department.

TAKE IT FURTHER: Film the speeches (in the same way that the popular TED talks are often filmed) and post the videos to the faculty or school YouTube account.

 ASSESSMENT: There are three main assessments for this project: the research report, the written speech and the spoken speech.

 21ST CENTURY LEARNING: Inter-cultural understanding, communication, ICT, critical thinking.

LITERACY: grammar – sentence types, clauses; punctuation – semicolon, commas, ellipses, dashes and brackets; reading – summarising, monitoring

MODE: writing and speaking

TYPE OF TEXT: persuasive

LANGUAGE FEATURES OF TEXTS: modality, connectives, emotive and figurative language, construction of an argument

POSSIBLE TEXTS: There is a wide range of TED and TEDx talks available via YouTube that will provide students with a good model for their speech.

HOW CAN WE USE MOBILE PHONES TO HELP US LEARN?

DISCOVER
Research mobile phones in education – pros and cons; language forms and features of persuasive texts

CREATE
A speech answering the driving question with PPT

SHARE
Speech in front of principal or head of department

BEFORE YOU BEGIN

CONTACT EXPERTS/ROCK STARS

This project requires students to share their learning with an online audience via YouTube. It is important you check that your students have the appropriate permissions to publish video and pictures of themselves online. If some students do not have permission – or if they are particularly shy – you can still include them by encouraging them to provide voice-overs, be in charge of costuming, props, sound effects or being the camera-person. If your faculty or school doesn't have a YouTube channel, now is a great time to create one. It's very easy and, ironically, there are a lot of YouTube tutorials to help you with the set-up.

This project also requires students to share their learning with the school principal. The principal of your school is a very important audience for this project, as students' discoveries and speeches about the use of mobile phones in education may have a positive real-world impact on the way students learn in your school. Who knows, maybe the school's policies about the use of mobile phones might change because of your students? It is a great idea to ask your principal to participate well in advance of when the presentations are due. Book in an exact date, time and location. This information should be shared with students at the very beginning of the project – it gives their learning purpose and focus.

MODIFY PROJECT OUTLINE

Now is the time to modify the given project outline. You may decide to change some of the key elements in order to meet the needs of your students. Look closely at the three stages of learning – discover, create, share – and consider what might need to be modified. Remember that PBL is all about engaging students through making content significant for their needs and interests. You will also need to modify the project outline to indicate due dates for formative and summative assessment.

ORGANISE PROJECT PACKETS

This is a relatively short project. It will probably only take three weeks for students to complete. The shorter the better, as this keeps the pressure on students to work each lesson. There are a number of resources that will be useful to include in these project packets, including:

- information on structure and language of persuasive texts. These resources should match the needs of your students and may take the form of worksheets or links to websites with interactive activities. Some students will require scaffolds to support their writing.
- information on speech writing and making. As with the above, this may simply take the form of a worksheet students complete using information from their own inquiry, or you may choose to give them specific information. This choice will depend on the skills of your students and your ability to access technology.
- team contract (you might like to use the proforma provided in Part 3: Additional Resources)
- checklist for persuasive speech writing
- checklist for YouTube video
- project calendar
- copy of project outline.

PLAN PROJECT TEAMS

This is a project where it is a good idea to ensure quite mixed teams. If you are running this project early in the school year, you may not know your students well enough to identify who has these skills. In this case, you may like to have students complete a self-assessment or a skills inventory prior to the project. The data from this assessment will help you with forming teams. Each team for this project will need to have:

- a confident public speaker, or two
- a confident technology user — to edit the YouTube video
- someone with really good ideas and strong opinions
- a team leader who will ensure all team members are on task.

We would suggest teams be no bigger than four. With a project like this, it might even be preferable to have teams of three. This will give each student the potential to contribute meaningfully to this project.

CREATE SPACE FOR A PROJECT WALL

Your project wall needs to be highly visible. If you don't have a home-room, you might like to seek permission from the school executive to use an external space, such as a wall outside of a classroom that you use for that class. Another alternative is to have a digital project wall. There are some great web tools to create these, such as Weebly and Glogster. These sites allow you to create interactive project walls, where students can click on the project outline and see it in greater detail, or access additional resources like scaffolds or checklists. Things to include on this project's wall:

- project outline
- project calendar
- key terms
- need to know
- project title
- project's driving question

As with all project walls, you will add to this wall as students progress through the project. If a team comes up with a great idea or creates something great, celebrate that by posting it to the project wall. Remember that this wall is a visual representation of student learning, so keep it bright, up to date and engaging.

LAUNCH YOUR PROJECT

HOOK LESSON

There are so many possibilities with this project. We know students love their mobile phones, but many schools don't permit students to use them as learning aids. If your school doesn't allow students to have their phones out in class, then you might need to run a role-play hook lesson that focuses on how students cope without their phones. Encourage them to use exaggerated dialogue and movement, even parody, to represent the struggle to exist without a phone. If your school does allow mobile phones in class — or if you're a bit of a rule breaker — then a lesson where students are asked to complete work ONLY using their phone would be super fun. Here are some possibilities:

- Have students create a song using the ring tones from the phones of all team members. This could be a round robin, a call and response or a discordant mash-up of multiple sounds (so post-modern.)
- Have students perform a skit where all of the dialogue is pre-recorded onto mobile phones and one student must play them at the appropriate moments in the skit.
- Take students outside and have them write poems about an object they can see — a pole, a rock, a tree and a garbage bin — and then take photographs to illustrate it. The poem and photos can then be posted to a social media site like Facebook or Twitter, or to a class blog, website or Edmodo group. This task can be done individually or in teams.

POSE DRIVING QUESTION

We like to think that students will really be engaged by this project. The content is highly significant to them and their experiences. The driving question for this project is the following.

HOW CAN MOBILE PHONES BE USED TO HELP US LEARN?

Write this question on the whiteboard and then have students use the 'Think/Pair/Share' thinking strategy to develop their initial thesis. This strategy asks students to sit quietly and write their own initial response to the question, then join with a partner to share their respective ideas. Finally, students join with another pair to form a quad, and they discuss their response to the driving question. One student from the quad will present the ideas to the class, which the teacher (or a nominated student scribe) will record on the whiteboard. The next activity gets students to decide on their own position, in light of the ideas of others. Have students create a 'human continuum' where they stand along an imagined line between 'NO' and 'YES'. It's inevitable that you will get bunches of students at one end or the other, so encourage them to really consider if they are 100% against or for the use of mobile phones being used to support learning. If they are unsure, tell them to spread out on the continuum a little. Once students have made their final decision, select students at random to justify their decision. This should end up with some lively discussions, but also reminds students that you need to be able to support your ideas with reasons and evidence. The final task for the lesson is to have the whole class brainstorming to generate reasons for and against the driving question, with the teacher or a student recording ideas on the whiteboard. For homework, have students write their own individual response to the driving question.

HAND OUT PROJECT OUTLINE

As with all projects, make sure that you print off the project outline in colour or print on coloured paper. Hand out the outline and have students sit quietly and read through it, using a pen or highlighter to identify any information that they feel they do not understand or that they have questions about. This is an essential step, as this information becomes part of what the class has identified as what they 'need to know'. Post a copy of the project outline to the project wall and have students keep a copy of the outline in their portfolios or project packets.

ESTABLISH NEED TO KNOW

Once students have considered the driving question and have read through the project outline, it is time to encourage them to ask a lot of questions. These questions will become the 'need to know' for the project. Have students record them in their books or you might prefer to record them as a class and put them onto the project wall. It is really important that you encourage students to ask questions about the key content and skills related to the project. This project especially will require students to discover the language and structure of persuasive texts as well as content relating to the use of mobile phones to support learning in high school. Clearly the skills relating to composing persuasive texts will be your priority as an English teacher, whereas the content will be more significant to your students. Try to gently direct them to ask quality questions about both content and skills. Remember that these questions should be a combination of open-ended questions (How, Why, If) and close questions (What, How, When). This will support your students' in-depth inquiry.

SET UP TEAMS

You need to have decided on the teams before you go into class. This is because this project requires quite a diverse range of skills. However, sometimes you may like to give students the freedom to select their own teams. We find that students are better equipped to do this in the second half of the school year, as they are more aware of their own and their peers' learning strengths. You might like to give each team a name and put this name on their team project packet. This makes it personal and fun for the students. It also shows that they are united as a team. One task that is useful at this early stage is to have students spend time identifying their own strengths and weaknesses as team members as well as their strengths and weaknesses in terms of the project. For example, a student might identify that she is good at public speaking but that she is easily distracted in class. Each student should share their personal strengths and weaknesses with the team so they can be discussed, and possible strategies for strengthening weaknesses considered. It is a good idea for you to keep a record of these strengths and weaknesses as well, because you can use them as the basis for assessing collaboration skills throughout the project.

CREATE A PROJECT CALENDAR

This project only has one main product — the persuasive speech addressing the driving question which is presented to your principal and filmed for YouTube. You may want to go in with a predetermined date for the final presentation, or you might want to negotiate this with the students. Either way, this needs to be the first thing that is put onto the project calendar. From this point, students will need to backwards-map how they will get to the end presentation. Spend some time in class negotiating this. Individual teams may choose to organise their time differently — more time on research or more time on presentation — and you should discuss the pros and cons of this approach. It is very important that the project calendar reflects opportunities for teams to receive feedback on their research and their draft speeches.

DISCOVER

GETTING TO KNOW THE RESEARCH

This project requires students to research the positives and negatives associated with using mobile phones for learning in high school. There are a number of research methods students can use:

- accessing the Internet to research both sides of the issue, looking at news articles, research papers and teacher blogs
- searching YouTube for videos about the ways in which mobile phones (and mobile devices such as tablets) have been used in high-school settings to support learning
- interviewing teachers at the school to ask their opinions on the topic
- surveying teachers from schools around the world using an online survey form such as Google Forms or Surveymonkey.com
- reflecting on their own personal experiences with mobile phones in the classroom.

GETTING TO KNOW THE STRUCTURE AND LANGUAGE OF PERSUASIVE SPEECHES

This project requires students to plan, draft and present a persuasive speech. Persuasive speeches have a specific structure and language features. There are a number of ways that you can support your students in developing their skills in persuasive writing, including:

- providing worksheets or handouts about the specific structure and language features
- providing models of well-written persuasive speeches for students to de-construct
- having students engage with interactive online tools
- showing YouTube videos about the specific structure and language features.

Remember that teaching any type of written text provides you with a great opportunity to model how to effectively use grammar and punctuation and to focus on specific spelling rules. A list of these that are relevant to persuasive speeches has been included on the opening page of this chapter.

You may wish to share this with your students.

FORMATIVE ASSESSMENT

This project focuses on writing and speaking skills, specifically argumentative and persuasive. Remember that PBL is about the process of learning as much as it is about the quality of the final product. Both speaking and writing require a lot of planning to ensure that the content is well-selected to support students' ideas. Having something to say is the first challenge of writing and ample time must be given to this stage. Formative assessment activities that you might use to support learning at this stage include:

- submission of research notes for teacher feedback
- brainstorming ideas using spider-maps
- selecting lines of argument and supporting evidence using mind-maps

MARKING CRITERIA: PERSUASIVE SPEECH

CRITERIA	EFFECTIVELY ACCOMPLISHED 10–8	PARTIALLY ACCOMPLISHED 6–4	NOT ACCOMPLISHED 0–2
CONTENT: AUDIENCE, PERSUASIVE DEVICES, IDEAS	<ul><li>The speech skilfully engages and persuades the audience</li><li>Excellent selection and elaboration of ideas relevant to the driving question</li><li>A wide variety of persuasive devices (such as rhetorical questions, personal voice, strong verbs and examples) have been used to enhance the writer's position and engage the reader</li></ul>	<ul><li>The speech engages and persuades the audience reasonably well</li><li>Sound selection and some elaboration of ideas relevant to the driving question</li><li>Attempts to use persuasive devices (such as rhetorical questions, personal voice, strong verbs and examples) to enhance the writer's position and engage the reader</li></ul>	<ul><li>The speech fails to engage and persuade the audience</li><li>Weak selection and minimal elaboration of ideas relevant to the driving question</li><li>Few persuasive devices have been used</li></ul>
MECHANICS: PUNCTUATION, SPELLING, SENTENCE STRUCTURE, VOCABULARY	<ul><li>A wide range of precise and appropriate language choices have been made – specifically vocabulary relevant to the speech topic</li><li>All sentences are grammatically correct, structurally sound and meaningful</li><li>All punctuation is correct</li><li>All words are spelled correctly including more complex and technical spelling words</li></ul>	<ul><li>Language choices are appropriate to the speech topic but lack detail</li><li>Most sentences are grammatically correct, structurally sound and meaningful</li><li>Most punctuation is correct but some errors</li><li>Most words are spelled correctly but some errors</li></ul>	<ul><li>Language choices may be inappropriate and not relevant to the speech topic</li><li>Sentences are unclear and contain obvious grammatical errors</li><li>Frequent punctuation errors</li><li>Frequent spelling errors and vocabulary is basic</li></ul>
FORM: TEXT STRUCTURE, PARAGRAPHING, COHESION	<ul><li>Highly effective structure appropriate to a speech including introduction, body and conclusion</li><li>All ideas are supported using evidence (anecdote, quote or personal observation)</li><li>Highly effective segmenting of the speech into paragraphs that assist the audience to follow the line of argument</li></ul>	<ul><li>Uses structure appropriate to a speech including introduction, body and conclusion but may be disorganised or too short</li><li>Most ideas are supported using evidence (anecdote, quote or personal observation)</li><li>Speech is segmented into paragraphs that assist the audience to follow the line of argument</li></ul>	<ul><li>Speech is missing some or all of the required structural components</li><li>Ideas are not supported using evidence</li><li>Speech is not divided into paragraphs or paragraphs are infrequent</li></ul>

CREATE

The composition for this project is a persuasive speech. By now, students should have a solid understanding of the language and structure of a persuasive speech, as well as the content for their speech. They will also have planned an outline for their speech, as a team. Core elements of quality PBL are revision and reflection. Drafting is an essential step in producing quality written work, just like rehearsing is an essential step in presenting a great speech.

WRITTEN PERSUASIVE SPEECH

In this project, students will begin by writing their draft persuasive speech as a team. Each team member will need to take responsibility for a specific line of argument, and write a body paragraph about it. The team should write the introduction and conclusion together.

SPOKEN PERSUASIVE SPEECH

Each team must negotiate which part of the speech each team member will be responsible for presenting. They will need to ensure that the transitions between speakers are smooth and that all speakers are presenting to the same standard.

The following page gives a detailed breakdown of language features of effective persuasive speeches.

FORMATIVE ASSESSMENT

This project provides students with a great opportunity to develop self and peer assessment skills in a non-threatening way. Here are a few useful strategies you may wish to use:

- Students should use the feedback checklist on the following page to assess their own paragraph and the paragraph of a friend.
- Teamwork should be assessed at this point. Use the strengths and weaknesses each student identified at the beginning of the project to provide students with feedback on their performance as team members.
- Students needs to be given lots of feedback on their speaking skills. Use the checklist provided to support them with this. You may want to spend time with each individual team, listening to their speeches and providing formative feedback using the criteria from the checklist.

HOW TO WRITE A PERSUASIVE SPEECH THAT ROCKS

LANGUAGE IS POWERFUL

That sentence is 100% the truth. The thing about powerful language is that it's even MORE powerful when it's spoken with passion. How do you write with power? Below are three sneaky tricks to giving some guts to your writing.

1. Repeat yourself. That's right, say the things you really, really care about more than once. You might want to repeat just a key word or a whole sentence. You might want to repeat an idea, but just say it slightly differently. If you don't believe me, have a look at some famous words from Martin Luther King Jnr:

   '**Let freedom ring** *from Stone Mountain of Georgia.*
   Let freedom ring *from Lookout Mountain of Tennessee.*
   Let freedom ring *from every hill and molehill of Mississippi.*'

2. Say it with certainty. People will believe you if you speak with conviction. The best way to do that is to make sure that the modality of your words is high. Modality is the level of certainty that you speak with – so when you're certain about something you might use the adverb 'absolutely' but if you're uncertain you might use the adverb 'perhaps'. Your job with this speech is to convince us, so let me hear you use some high modality language. Here's JFK being certain:

   '*I* **do not** *shrink from this responsibility – I welcome it. I* **do not** *believe that any of us would exchange places with any other people or any other generation.*'

3. Ask questions to which you already know the answers. Sounds weird, right? Well, rhetorical questions are designed to make people think, and that's what you want your speech to do. Think of provocative questions about your topic that you know will force your audience to question themselves and their thoughts about mobile phones. Former Prime Minister Julia Gillard used a series of rhetorical questions in her attack on the Opposition Leader Tony Abbott's misogyny:

   '*Well, can anybody remind me if the Leader of the Opposition has taken any responsibility for the conduct of the Sydney Young Liberals and the attendance at this event of members of his front bench? Has he taken any responsibility for the conduct of members of his political party and members of his front bench who apparently, when the most vile things were being said about my family, raised no voice of objection?*'

SHARE

This will be a nerve-wracking event for you and your students. Presenting in front of the principal puts your teaching talents in the spotlight – although it should always just be about the students and their learning. Make sure you dedicate at least two lessons to running through the speeches, focusing on the order in which each team presents. You will also need to make sure that you have one or more students prepped on how to use the video camera to record the speeches. Sound is very important. Make sure you test the quality of the sound before the day of the presentations. You may need to use an external microphone. It is a good idea to film a rehearsal of each team. This activity will provide a great source of feedback for students as they will be able to watch their performance and identify strengths and weaknesses. A nice addition would be to have students using their mobile phones to help them present – as clickers for their presentation, using the stopwatch to help them keep time or to record their speech. Have them think of creative ways to incorporate their mobile phones.

On the day of the speeches, have one student introduce the project and explain it briefly. Make sure that you provide writing paper, a glass of water and some sweets for the principal – this informs your students that you take their learning seriously and that they are professionals.

You may wish to sit at a table with the principal, and use the teacher checklist to give students feedback on their final performance. This is essentially the summative assessment for this project. It is optional. If you and your school are happy for students to focus entirely on the process and their learning, don't focus heavily on the final speech. Often students are putting pressure on themselves because they want the project to be a success. This is only going to be the case if students value their learning and see it as having meaning in their world. This project makes this likely, since their principal may actually alter school policy based on their presentations. Furthermore, their speeches may impact on the decisions made at other schools if their YouTube videos are shared with a wider audience.

POST-PROJECT REFLECTION/EVALUATION

This project, like all projects, requires students to reflect on their learning. This can be done as a class discussion, where you sit together in a circle and talk about what they loved and what they didn't love about the project. Perhaps you might like to use a PMI table to evaluate the project. One has been included on the next page for you to use. This makes the focus on the project itself – so that means you – which requires you to be open to criticism. This is hard at first, because having students critique your work is probably an unfamiliar experience. We've found it to be a very liberating experience as well as a productive strategy to improve the way we teach. Another important reflection for this project is individual student reflection. Ask them to look back at their personal strengths and weaknesses as a team member that they identified early in the project. It is now time for them to consider each, and reflect on a time where they used their strengths to support their group's learning, and a time when they worked hard to overcome their weaknesses to avoid negatively impacting on learning.

MOBILE LEARNING: PROJECT EVALUATION

PLUS	MINUS	INTERESTING

YEAR 9

3. SPEAK UP

PROJECT AT A GLANCE

 **DRIVING QUESTION:** How can one voice change the world?

 DISCOVER: Students will be reading, listening to and viewing performance poetry from a range of contexts and genres.

 CREATE: Students will be writing individual and group performance poems. They will also individually write an analytical essay on two poems they have studied.

 SHARE: Students will plan and run a Slam Poetry evening where they will perform their poetry in front of an audience of family, friends and local poets.

TAKE IT FURTHER: Filmed performances of each individual OR team poem can be posted to the faculty or school YouTube channel.

 ASSESSMENT: Three pieces of completed work will be assessed in this project: the analytical essay, individual poem and the team poem.

 21ST-CENTURY SKILLS: inter-cultural understanding, ethical understanding, creative thinking, collaboration and communication

LITERACY: grammar – ellipses, connectives; spelling – creative spelling (voice and character); punctuation – commas, dashes; reading – visualising and making connections

LANGUAGE FEATURES OF TEXTS: poetic devices, rhetorical questions, repetition, refrain, verse, allusion and evocative vocabulary

POSSIBLE TEXTS: http://protestpoemsdotorg.blogspot.com.au

How Can One Voice Change the World?

Discover
- a variety of performance poets and their poems
- the language, structure and styles distinctive to performance poets
- the language critique

Assessment:

Due:

Create
- a theatrical performance of a poem of your choice
- an original performance poem about an issue in the news you feel passionate about

Assessment:

Due:

Share
- your original composition with an online audience
- your choice of performance poem for friends and family at a 'SLAM Poetry' evening

Assessment:

Due:

BEFORE YOU BEGIN

CONTACT EXPERTS

This project requires students to plan, draft, rehearse and then perform protest poems before an audience of family, friends and invited guests. This will require a lot of initial planning. While it is important to allow students to organise the event itself – booking a venue, organising the catering and creating invitations – you will need to take responsibility for inviting the guest experts. Who are the experts that you could invite? There are a range of possibilities:

- an academic from a local university who specialises in contemporary poetry
- a slam poet who has entered one of the many slam poetry events that run in Australia
- a published poet who lives in the local area
- an amateur poet you have connected with via social media
- a poet from the Red Room Company
- an international poet who might Skype in with your students or communicate with them via Twitter at the initial research stage of the project
- a representative from the local youth council or similar youth organisation

You may wish to invite your guest expert to speak with your students at the initial research stage, and invite them back for the final performance. You may choose to have one expert come at the beginning of the project (perhaps the academic) and another come for the final performance (perhaps the amateur poet).

HOOK LESSON

The hook lesson for this project can focus on two main aspects of the project: the content (controversial issues worthy of protest) or the form (performance poetry). The list below has suggestions for hook lessons that could be used to engage students in this project:

- watch performance poets on YouTube (we really like 'Theatre' by Rik Mayall and 'Play On' by Omar Musa)
- 3-minute debates where teams are given a controversial issue to debate
- watch film clips of protest songs
- stage a mini school protest about school-related issues, with signs and chants

DISCOVER

The discover stage of learning will see your students engaging closely with a range of poetry. You may choose to engage with the poems as a whole class, or give each team time to discuss, analyse and evaluate a given poem and present their learning to the class. We recommend a combination of the two. Firstly model how to engage critically with a poem through a whole-class discussion and co-construction of an analytical paragraph, evaluating the poem's strength and weaknesses. In this instance, focus on the use of poetic devices (a suggested list has been given on the project overview page) and performance techniques such as pitch, pace, pause, tone, inflection, facial expressions, gestures and body language. Next, allocate each team with a performance poem (try to choose a range of issues such as racism, bullying, sexism, war and the environment) and have them complete a similar analysis they then present for the class. Encourage them to use ICT to support their presentation – this might include PowerPoint, Powtoon or Prezi. You might like to give students the worksheet on the next page to support their analysis of the poem. A one-page worksheet with activities for students to complete in this discovery stage has been included if you feel your students require more structure.

FORMATIVE ASSESSMENT

There are a number of different formative assessment strategies that you may choose to use to check students' understanding of the structure and language features of performance poems. What follows is a list of some that you may choose to use.

- Poetic devices quiz. This should be quick and presented in a non-threatening manner. Ensure students have time to prepare for the quiz because it can cause anxiety in some students if they are given a quiz without warning.
- Daily exit slips. For this stage of the project, you might wish to focus on content such as identifying specific poetic devices or answering two or three questions about a poem.
- Think, puzzle and explore blog posts. This is a homework activity where students write a 100–200 word blog post, identifying something that the poems made them think about, or that puzzled them or something they would like to explore further.
- Writing an analytical paragraph about a poem. This writing task will be modelled and scaffolded to support students. Look at students' work to identify weaknesses that need to be addressed through further inquiry or teacher support.
- KWL table. As with all projects, the initial stage sees students identify their learning needs through writing 'need to know' questions. Looking through these will help you to determine which student will need greater support during the project.

SPEAK UP INQUIRY ACTIVITIES

POWERFUL ISSUES

What is there to protest about in our world today? List as many issues you can think of that you believe are worthy of protesting for or against.

HISTORICAL PROTEST MOVEMENTS

Select one historical protest movement and write a 300-word description of it. Your description should include why the protest started, how it developed and how it ended. Be sure to include references to key figures. You might like to search 'protest movements'. Include a Reference List that shows all sources.

PROTEST SONG – ANALYSIS

a. Read the lyrics to Pink Floyd's 'Another Brick in the Wall' and complete the following as a team:

1. Identify WHAT the song is protesting against. (1 sentence)
2. Explain HOW the composer tries to communicate this message. (2 poetic techniques and an example for each – 4 sentences)
3. Evaluate how EFFECTIVELY each technique helps to communicate the writer's protest. Think about what they want you to think/feel/imagine. (2 sentences – one for each poetic technique identified.)
4. Judge the RELEVANCE of this protest to humanity – why should we care about it? (1–2 sentences.)

b. Select from one of the songs below and complete an individual analysis of it, using the questions above as a guide:

- Grandmaster Flash – The Message
- Bliss n Eso – Bullet & A Target
- Rage Against the Machine – Guerilla Radio
- The Cranberries – Zombie
- Christina Aguilera – Beautiful

RESPONDING TO A PROTEST POEM

CONTEXT: make some notes about the times, values and concerns of the poet and how they are evident in the poem's themes or style.

PURPOSE: What is the purpose of the poem?

ISSUES AND CONCERNS: State what the issues or concerns are and discuss how these reflect the times or context of the poet.

TONE: Describe the tone. Are there any shifts in tone? What words/phrases help to convey the tone?

LANGUAGE FEATURES: Identify them, comment on their impact on the reader/listener and why the poet uses them.

VOCALS: Describe the pace, delivery, tone, instruments (if relevant) etc.

YOUR PERSONAL RESPONSE: Do you agree or disagree with what is being said and do you feel that the poet effectively conveys his or her message?

WHAT IDEAS IS THE POEM EXPRESSING?	WHAT POETIC TECHNIQUE IS BEING USED TO SAY THIS?	WHAT IS AN EXAMPLE OF THIS TECHNIQUE BEING USED?	WHAT DOES THIS TECHNIQUE MAKE YOU THINK, FEEL OR IMAGINE RELATING TO THE IDEAS OF THE POEM?	WHY IS THIS IDEA IMPORTANT TO PEOPLE IN THE WORLD? RESTATE THE MAIN IDEA OF THE POEM
The devastation and destruction caused by war is being protested against by Wilfred Owen in his poem *Dulce Et Decorum Est*.	Simile	'Bent double, like old beggars under sacks, Knock-kneed, coughing like hags, we cursed through sludge'	Creates a disturbing image of the young soldiers transformed into weary old men as a result of their experiences in the war.	Wars continue to wage around the world, resulting in the needless deaths of many young people. Owen masterfully crafts a series of images in his poem that reveal the true devastation and destruction caused by war.
	(Furthermore) Onomatopoeia	'If you could hear, at every jolt, the blood Come gargling from the froth-corrupted lungs'	Captures a horrific aural image of painful death and evokes sympathy for the young soldiers who suffer such a tragic fate.	

Name the Poetic Technique

You have been a range of sentences, each containing a specific poetic technique. Write the poetic device that has been used next to the example.

You eat like a pig. ....

You are a pig. ....

Ladies like lovely lipstick. ....

The fingers of the vine grabbed at her hair. ....

As blind as a bat. ....

The rain in Spain stays mainly on the plain. ....

The bug crunched under his thumping boot. ....

'All the world's a stage and all the men and women merely players.' ....

'Life is like a box of chocolates, you never know what you're gonna get.' ....

The siren wailed. ....

Her eyes they shone like diamonds. ....

He wolfed down his dinner. ....

The river was choking on the rubbish. ....

Slowly, silently and stealthily he crept. ....

You missed the target by a mile. ....

He was a wise fool. ....

As the battle reached its climax, the terrifying storm erupted in the sky. ....

CREATE 🎵

In this project students will discover ideas relating to a specific controversial issue of their choosing, as well as the structure and language features of performance poetry. Students will also be developing their performance skills. This can be quite daunting for some students, so make sure you create a really supportive, non-threatening learning environment for your students so they feel confident enough to take risks and try something new.

PERFORMING A POEM

Each team should be given or should select a poem to perform for the class. They may also, potentially, perform at their Slam Poetry evening. Students will need to be encouraged to look closely at the role that punctuation plays in their given poem – encourage them to annotate the poem to identify appropriate places for:

- pauses
- emphasis
- volume
- gestures
- body language
- facial expressions.

To enhance their performance, students may wish to incorporate costumes, music or sound effects, make-up and props. Obviously they will need to make sure that these choices are appropriate to the mood and content of their given/chosen poem.

COMPOSING A TEAM PERFORMANCE POEM

Students will need to spend some time with their team brainstorming controversial topics about which they could write a poem. Another possibility is that you may like to brainstorm a long list of topics as a class, and then allow teams time to select one from that list. Once students have selected their team's topic, time will need to be given for them to research information about that topic. It's important that the speech is passionate, heartfelt and (possibly) a call to action. Performance poetry is about raising awareness of an issue or of an individual's personal experiences. These poems tend to be focused on social justice issues and aim to change the attitudes and opinions of the listener. As such, it is pertinent that students select a topic that they feel some genuine passion for, or possibly have personal experience of, and then research the issue further to help develop a powerful message about their chosen topic.

When students have come to the stage where they are ready to write, suggest that they read or listen to more performance poems to help them decide what type they like best. They will need to decide on the following:

- Will the poem be literal or symbolic?
- Will the poem have an obvious narrative, or will it be fragments of narratives?
- Who will be the speaker? Will there be multiple speakers, presenting multiple perspectives on the issue?
- What type of rhythm and rhyme scheme will be the most suitable for their topic?
- What will be the mood of the poem? For example, sad, angry, hurt, proud, or will it feature shifting moods?

- How will imagery be used to communicate their message about the issue?
- Will the poem have a refrain or repetition?

Be sure to allow time for planning, where lots of ideas are put forward, as well as adequate time to receive teacher feedback on the written poem.

FORMATIVE ASSESSMENT

Below are some strategies you might like to use to check students' understanding and skills at this stage of the project.

- Checklist for performance of a poem: a great activity is to have students develop the criteria for their product. In this instance, they will be performing a poem that has been written by someone else. Students should have a good knowledge of what makes a great performance, as they have engaged with the performance poetry of others in the discover stage of learning. Brainstorm 5–10 features that a great performance poem must have. Use these to create a checklist for success. A blank checklist has been included for you in 'Part 3: Additional Resources'.

- 30-second check-ins. This formative assessment strategy is useful when students are working collaboratively in their teams to compose their performance poems. Select a time during the lesson and stop students working. Ask for silence. Choose one student from each team to stand up in front of the class and, in thirty seconds, share what their team is working on. Encourage them to share what they have achieved, what they have learned and what they still need to do in order to successfully complete their team performance poem.

- Use the checklist for a performance poem (written) resource to give each team quality, timely and meaningful feedback on the first draft of their poem.

- Have students look at the sample poem 'Infamous and Irreversible'. Ask them to evaluate its effectiveness, focusing on content, mood, structure and style.

Infamous and Irreversible

By Angus Buckley

In a room, you will find no pink walls or purple door
You will find a dark place written with signs of civil war
Beneath your bed, enveloped in fright
Hidden in the gutters till they appear in the night
They're those petrifying stories your parents told you in bed
That succeeded failure to escape your head
Those were stories of the people painted black,
And infamous White Cloaks who planned to attack.
The White Brotherhood are demons sent from hell,
Given the mission to convey a spell
They will show no mercy till they've got their way,
And will show no remorse till they've crippled their prey.
There are several colours within a rainbow
Yet these cone-headed brutes believe they stand alone.
The change of one voice could be the change of many,
And the form that this could take could be any.
We should not waste our time to ponder and be contrite
For what this time should be used for is for all to unite.

Protest Form

Name: **Teacher:**

Criteria/Skill (goals)	Self-assessment			Teacher Assessment
	I didn't	I think I did	I did	
Does your poem explore a controversial topic or social justice issue you feel passionately about?				
Does your poem include a call to action, or encourage readers to change their attitude to your chosen topic?				
Did you use poetic structure to effectively communicate your ideas?				
Did you create a distinctive and emotive voice for your speaker(s)?				
Have you used repetition or a refrain to reinforce your main message?				
Did you use correct spelling?				
Did you use correct punctuation? (Especially for dialogue.)				
Did you use a variety of sentence types to create pace and mood?				
Did you use tense and narrative voice consistently?				
Did you use figurative language, verbs, adjectives and adverbs to create visual and aural imagery?				

Main strengths: (medals)

Improvements needed for this essay: (missions)

Self-assessed target: (missions)	Targets for the next essay: (missions)

SHARE

Students will need to spend at least three lessons planning and rehearsing the performance of their poems. Remind them to look back at what they learned about effective performance when they performed a poem written by someone else.

To enhance their performance, students may wish to incorporate costumes, music or sound effects, make-up and props. Obviously they will need to make sure that these choices are appropriate to the mood and content of their given/chosen poem.

Encourage students to get involved with organising the SLAM poetry evening. They should give the event a catchy name — as silly as it seems, this will make it more valuable for your students. Give them some time to create flyers or invitations as well as posters or decorations for the venue. Instruct students to bring a plate of food as refreshments for the guests. You will also need to double-check that the guest expert and other invited guests are still able to attend the evening.

FORMATIVE ASSESSMENT

Below are some strategies you might like to use to check students' understanding and skills at this stage of the project.

- It is important that students get feedback on their performance at least once before the final event. You might like to use the performance checklist created by the students earlier in the project for when they performed the poem written by someone else.
- After the performances, have each student write on a slip of paper which team performance they enjoyed the most, giving two reasons why they selected that team. Encourage them to support their selection with reasons from the criteria used for a performance poem.

YEAR 9
4. TEENS UNITE

PROJECT AT A GLANCE

 **DRIVING QUESTION:** How can we support teenagers who are finding life hard?

 DISCOVER: Students will read a novel that explores teenage experiences and spend time analysing its writing style and themes. Students will also research the experiences of teenagers in other countries and write a report on their findings to share on the class website. Finally, students will research ways to support young people in their local area.

 CREATE: Students will individually write a review of the prescribed novel. In small teams students will create a visual representation of one issue confronting youth today. This will include a rationale to justify their creative choices.

 SHARE: Individual students will publish their novel review on a website such as Goodreads or Amazon. The visual representations will be showcased at an exhibition held in the school hall for parents and community members.

 ASSESSMENT: Pieces of work to be assessed are the research report, novel review and visual representation.

 21ST-CENTURY SKILLS: critical thinking, creative thinking, ICT, ethical understanding

LITERACY: grammar – lexical cohesion, modality, abstraction, grammatical theme, sentence and clause structures; reading – identify, explain and discuss narrative viewpoint

MODE: reading, writing and representing/creating

TYPE OF TEXT: informative (report), persuasive (visual rep), imaginative (novel)

LANGUAGE FEATURES OF TEXTS: narrative structure, theme, figurative language, narrative voice

POSSIBLE TEXT CHOICES: *The Fault in Our Stars*; *Looking for Alibrandi, The Catcher in the Rye, Deadly, Unna?*

How can we help teenagers who are having a tough time?

Discover
- the life experiences of other teenagers
- how to support teenagers locally, nationally and globally

Create
- a visual representation of the issues confronting teenagers around the world

Share
- your representations at an exhibition

BEFORE YOU BEGIN

CONTACT EXPERTS

This is an issues-based project. Students will be engaged in meaningful research into issues that negatively impact on the lives and well-being of teenagers around the world. They will then spend time considering solutions and ways to advocate for positive changes to make the lives of teenagers better. During the inquiry stage, students should connect with teenagers living in other parts of the world. This will give authenticity to their inquiry and to the project as a whole. You can connect with other classes by networking with other teachers via social media sites such as Twitter, Facebook, Edmodo and Skype. The final presentation is before a public audience. Take some time to get in contact with local stakeholders who have a say in the way that young people are supported in your community. These may include the mayor, local MPs, youth workers, local businesspeople and family members.

PLAN THE PROJECT LAUNCH

- Turn your classroom into a picture gallery by displaying a range of images of teenagers from around the world on classroom walls or other spaces. When students enter the room, give them four or five Post-It notes. They are to look at all the images and then select the ones that make them THINK, FEEL or IMAGINE what it is like to be a teenager in a different context to their own. They write the appropriate verb at the top of the Post-It and then write a sentence explaining what they think, feel or imagine when they look at the image. For example, a recruitment poster might elicit feelings of bravery or patriotism. Songs about teenage experience (such as 'At Seventeen', 'Teenage Riot', 'Smells Like Teen Spirit', 'Teenage Lobotomy') are played while the students walk silently through the gallery. (Teacher will need to remind students of appropriate behaviour for a gallery.)
- Generate a big list of things that make life hard for teenagers and ways of dealing with these hard times.
- Spend the lesson reminiscing about childhood by reading picture books, watching cartoons, and eating biscuits and drinking milk.

DISCOVER

The first couple of weeks for this project will have students spending time reading a novel that explores the difficult experiences of young people living in a context vastly different to their own. This is a great opportunity to develop students' empathy and to have them thinking about the ethical decisions faced by others their own age. You may choose to read the novel aloud as a class, or have students read at home and then spend time discussing as a class. Either way, this stage of the project requires students to consider the themes of the novel and how the author has used structure and writing style to communicate these themes to their readers. Students may want to record their discoveries on a worksheet or table (similar to the sample provided), on a collaborative document or in their workbooks.

The purpose of the discovery stage is for your students to come away with an appreciation of the similarities and differences between the life experiences of teenagers around the world, focusing primarily on what might make life difficult for teenagers in each context. The following is a list of other possible learning activities for your students at the discovery stage of the project.

- Watch a documentary about teenagers living in another country and discuss themes and techniques.
- Connect with a class from another country. This could include making a series of videos where each class shares their experiences of being a teenager, or perhaps each class could complete a survey about their life experiences. To do this use sites like ePals, Skype in the Classroom, Edmodo or Twitter.
- Research problems confronted by teenagers in their own country, especially those who come from a different culture or demographic.
- Research problems confronted by teenagers in their local community.
- Write a report on what they have learned, answering the driving question.

FORMATIVE ASSESSMENT TIPS

Below are some strategies you might like to use to check students' understanding and skills at this stage of the project.

- report posted to class website to be assessed for student understanding and the quality of research
- check the quality of the 'need to know' questions to assess understanding
- quality of collaborative behaviours such as sharing ideas, contributing to team discussions and team tasks.

CHAPTER AND PAGE NUMBER	CONFLICT/ OBSTACLE FACED	RESPONSE TO CONFLICT/ OBSTACLE OUTCOME (+/–)	HOW WAS THIS COMMUNICATED: CHARACTERISATION, STRUCTURE, VOICE, MOTIF, SYMBOLS, VISUAL ELEMENTS, FIGURATIVE LANGUAGE, DIALOGUE, MOOD, THEME, IMAGERY	LESSONS LEARNED

REPRODUCIBLE – PART TWO: SAMPLE PROJECTS YEAR 9 – 4. TEENS UNITE

CREATE 🎵

In teams, pairs or individually, students will create a visual representation answering the project's driving question. This task gives students much needed choice, as they are given the choice of which visual form they will create. Some options include picture book, diorama, flyers, posters, comic, documentary or short film. Please note that if students choose to create a short film or documentary they will need to devote a lot of time at home to completing it. Students are to ground their representation in the research they have conducted about the problems confronted by teenagers around the world. It is essential that students keep in mind their:

- Audience – people attending the exhibition, including parents, community members, teachers and politicians
- Context – a school hall, therefore they need to think carefully about how they present sensitive issues
- Purpose – to raise awareness of the difficulties facing young people around the world, to advocate for acknowledgment of young people's contributions and to seek additional funding for those in need.

The visual representation should be accompanied by a rationale in which students explain their ideas and justify their stylistic choices. This will assist them at the exhibition, when they will likely be asked by attendees to explain their visual representation.

FORMATIVE ASSESSMENT

Below are some strategies you might like to use to check students' understanding and skills at this stage of the project.

- Peer and/or self assessment of draft visual representation and rationale using a checklist
- Gallery walk for plans of visual representations. A gallery walk is where student work (usually drafts or plans) is set out around the room, and the class quietly walks around giving feedback via Post-It notes.

SHARE 👥

The dream with this project is that students will see themselves as active agents in their world, as well as appreciating the ways in which novels can capture the true experiences of individuals and inspire people to make a difference in the lives of others. At the final presentation, encourage your students to focus on:

- the need to better promote existing resources, spaces and programs to support young people in the local area;
- the need to create new, safe spaces for young people to come together, as well as opportunities for young people to give back to their community;
- the need to champion the achievements of young people.

As a class the students will need to plan a presentation that opens their exhibition – this will need to be visual and emotive. This presentation needs to appeal to the audience and be powerful enough to cause real change in their world.

To prepare for this stage of the project, students will need to do the following:
- organise the display of visual representations in the venue (likely a school hall or library) the day before
- check that videos run on laptops or tablets (for students who have created films or documentaries)
- call and check that special guests know the time and venue for the event – this should be done at least a week before the exhibition
- make a list of who is bringing a plate of food or drinks for refreshments

FORMATIVE ASSESSMENT TIPS

Below are some strategies you might like to use to check students' understanding and skills at this stage of the project.
- 30-second share: randomly select up to 10 students to share their learning for that lesson in a 30-second summary.
- Run a rehearsal of the mini speech each student will give at his or her exhibit to ensure everyone feels confident. You might like to have a trial question and answer session to prepare students for being asked questions about their exhibit.

YEAR 9
5. MIDNIGHT SNACKS

PROJECT AT A GLANCE

 **DRIVING QUESTION:** How can we compose a fantasy story that will interest eight-year-olds?

 DISCOVER: Students will read, view and interact with a variety of fantasy texts. They will also research the history of the fantasy genre and connect with students in a Year 2 class via Edmodo and Skype to discover their interests.

 CREATE: In teams, students will collaborate on a 3000-word fantasy story to be illustrated by the Year 2 students.

 SHARE: The collected stories written by the class will be published in an anthology using Blurb and will be given to the Year 2 class. Students will read excerpts of their stories to the Year 2 students in person or via Skype.

 ASSESSMENT: The individual report on two fantasy texts and the team short story will be assessed.

 21ST-CENTURY SKILLS: ICT, digital citizenship, communication, collaboration, critical thinking

LITERACY: grammar – phrases (group/phrase – verbs, nouns, adverbs, adjectives); spelling – multi-syllable words, suffixes; reading – making connections and visualising

MODE: reading, writing and viewing

TYPE OF TEXT: informative (report) and imaginative (story, range of texts)

LANGUAGE FEATURES OF TEXTS: characterisation, narrative structure, setting, genre and motif

POSSIBLE TEXTS: *The Hobbit* (novel or films); *Skyrim: Chronicles of Narnia; Alice in Wonderland; The Dark Crystal; The Labyrinth; The Never Ending Story.*

How can we compose a Fantasy Story that will interest eight-year-olds?

Discover

- history of fantasy genre
- conventions and features of fantasy genre
- the interests of eight-year-olds

Create

- work in a small team to plan, draft, edit and publish a fantasy story for eight-year-olds in collaboration with Year 2 students
- story must be no less than 2000 words in length

Share

- publish completed story (with accompanying Year 2 illustrations) in a hard-cover copy of collected fantasy stories
- present final products to Year 2

Some things you will learn

- features and conventions of fantasy texts
- how to write for a specific audience
- how to manage your time and work to a deadline
- the process of design: generating ideas, refining ideas, developing a draft, seeking feedback and editing.

BEFORE YOU BEGIN

CONTACT EXPERTS

This project requires that you take a risk and connect with people from outside of your school. If you don't, the project won't work. Why not? Well, the Year 2 students are actually the co-authors of the stories that your students are writing and they are also the audience for the final product. Connecting with others can be a bit stressful, but once you get to know the people you are connecting with it becomes a source of excitement and engagement for your students. Some things to think about initially are whether you'd like to connect with a local school or a school that is in another state or even another country. If you already have connections with a primary school teacher, then try to organise to work with them. If you think your students will be more motivated by meeting students from interstate or overseas, then social media is your friend. Use your connections via Facebook, Twitter, Edmodo or your blog to find a suitable class to work with you on the project. You will then use these channels to keep in contact with the other class and its teacher. We've found that there are many teachers willing to get their classes involved in creative projects such as this one. Be brave, ask around and you will find your bravery will be rewarded.

PLAN THE HOOK LESSON

Writing fantasy stories should be an engaging yet challenging experience for your students. They will likely have grown up being exposed to a whole range of fantasy stories through books, television, film and video games. To pique their interest in this project, you could use any of the following activities.

- A series of fun games including fantasy character "celebrity head", matching the character to their fantasy world and matching the author to the fantasy novel
- Storytelling games. These might include writing one sentence at a time stories, where students write a sentence on a piece of paper, fold it over and pass it to another student to write a sentence. This continues until the end of the piece of paper. Stories end up being ridiculous but funny. In a story cubes dice game (you can buy these in toy shops and book shops) each dice has a little picture on it, and students roll the dice and then must tell a story based on the images that they roll. Or you might have students select – at random – a character, setting and complication that they must use to tell a story through mime or tableaux.

PROJECT CALENDAR

PROJECT: MIDNIGHT SNACKS   DATES: 12/11/12 – 30/11/12

MONDAY	TUESDAY	WEDNESDAY	THURSDAY	FRIDAY
PROJECT WEEK ONE				
12/11	13/11	14/11	15/11 – learnt about elements of fantasy.	16/11 – post questions to Year 2.
PROJECT WEEK TWO				
19/11 – plan story in response to Year 2 answers.	20/11	21/11 – continue planning	22/11 – start writing story (negotiate roles)	23/11 – continue writing draft – send a post to Year 2 outlining story asking for feedback
PROJECT WEEK THREE				
26/11 – continue writing draft	27/11	28/11 – continue writing draft	29/11 – submit draft on Edmodo	30/11 – editing story

DISCOVER

A partially completed KWL table has been included for this stage of the project. My students completed this table on the second lesson of the project, just after they were given the project outline. Hopefully seeing my students' ideas will help you to see how students should be supported to generate their own questions about the project. A completed project calendar has been included as well – all information and dates were negotiated as a whole class in the second lesson of the project. It is quite compact and would be better suited to a longer period of time, however sometimes a shorter time period can focus students better as they see the deadline more clearly.

Students will need to do some research into the origins of the fantasy genre and try to get a sense of the conventions relating to it. This can be done through accessing information on the Internet or in reference books. You may wish to support students' research by giving them a scaffold for their findings. Students will write a 300-word micro report summarising their findings – request that they include references for at least three different sources. This is a great time to run a short, explicit lesson on quality Internet research and triangulating information. PBL provides students with the perfect opportunities to learn the importance of thinking critically about information.

The part of this inquiry stage of the project is to engage with a range of fantasy texts. Your students should have identified this as an essential 'need to know' when you first presented them with the project outline. Engaging with a wide range of fantasy stories in a range of forms will help students identify the shared conventions used by composers but also appreciate the subtle differences. Remind them that they need to know this because they will be composing their own fantasy stories very soon. You may wish to give the 'genre research task' worksheet to your students to help them record their findings about each text they respond to. Remember, you may choose to respond to some texts as a whole class – such as a film – but you may also set students the task of engaging with fantasy texts of their own choosing as well.

FORMATIVE ASSESSMENT

Below are some strategies you might like to use to check students' understanding and skills at this stage of the project.

- short quiz on the history and conventions of the fantasy genre
- teacher feedback on history and conventions of the fantasy genre reports
- self-assessment using SOLO taxonomy (see 'Part Three: Additional Resources' for more information)

What I Know	What I Wonder/Want to Know	What I Learned
We have to write a fantasy story for an eight-year-old.	Who will be the characters? (Elves? dwarves? magicians? orcs?)	
Fantasy includes mythical creatures such as dragons.	Where will it be set?	
The story needs to be a minimum of 2000 words.	What structure can I use in my story?	
We will be working in teams of three.	What interests eight-year-olds?	
We will be presenting the book of collected stories to the primary school students.	Are we going to meet the eight-year-olds?	
	How will we find out what they like to read?	
	Do we get some help to draw the illustrations?	
	Will the story be split into sections so each person writes their own part?	
The story needs to be suitable for boys and girls.	Is it going to be placed in their library?	
The story is going to be published in hard cover.	When is this all due?	
	What is the word limit?	
	Is a happy ending necessary?	
	What are the limits of fantasy?	
We will be focusing on ISTE NETS (1 and 4) and Habits of Mind (11, 15, 14)	Can we use dialogue?	
	How many copies are being published?	
	Is it to be written in first or third person?	
	How will it be published?	
We can get our ideas from other sources — like books, games and films.	Should we have bad or good characters?	
	How do we write a story that makes sense to an eight-year-old?	
	What is the mood of the story?	
Eight-year-olds will be illustrating the story.	When do we get to ask the eight-year-olds what they like in a story?	
We will need to seek and use peer feedback and feedback from the Year 2 students.	Do we type it up or write it in our book?	
	Why are we doing this?	
	Why is it targeted at Year 2s?	
The story will be fiction.	What will the eight-year-olds think about the book?	
Everyone likes unicorns.	How do we make a story appropriate for eight-year-olds?	
The story needs to be interesting.	How do we write a fantasy story?	
	Can we make money from it?	
	How much can an eight-year-old read?	
	How many eight-year-olds do we get to work with?	
	Are we allowed to use *some* complicated words?	
	What roles do the teams need to have?	

Genre Research Tasks

Title of Text:

Composer of Text:

Text form:

Brief overview of content:

Relevance of text to your project's concept:

Relevance of text to your project's audience:

Relevance of text to your project's form:

CREATE 🎵

The first part of this stage of the project is actually more inquiry. Now that your students have a solid understanding of the fantasy genre, it's time for them to meet their co-authors and their audience – the Year 2 students. The first task will be for your students to work out what interests eight-year-olds. They may like to hold a Skype question and answer discussion with the Year 2 class or they could create a survey for them to complete. The language will need to be accessible for eight-year-olds. Year 2 are the co-authors of these stories, therefore they need to be given the chance to contribute to the planning stages. Interacting via an online site such as Edmodo or Google Docs, the Year 2 students should share their ideas for characters, settings and action. Remind your students that they are writing this story FOR the Year 2 students, and therefore they need to respect and value the suggestions given – otherwise they will have very unhappy customers. This is a really fun part of the project, as your students will soon realise that eight-year-olds have fantastic imaginations.

Try to spend quality time with each team as they begin planning their fantasy story based on the ideas of the Year 2 students. This is a collaborative writing task, and that can be very hard for some students. It's essential that all students' contributions are valued equally. We've found that getting students to graphically represent their plot is a really effective way to plan. Encourage them to create a plot diagram on A3 or butcher paper that is clearly labelled, indicating elements such as the orientation, backfill, rising action, complication, resolution and coda (if applicable). If you have students who wish to subvert the traditional narrative structure, that's great, but it's still recommended that they plan in a traditional way first and then move the elements around later. Have students annotate their plan further to show which aspects of the narrative will conform to the conventions of the fantasy genre. On another piece of paper, have students create character portraits for the main character(s) and side character(s). They should give as much detail as possible – remind them that not all this detail will be directly referenced in the story, but knowing a lot about a character will make for a stronger story. This activity would be enhanced with contributions from the Year 2 students, so perhaps your students might want to write a series of questions about each character for the Year 2 students to answer. Breaking down the planning process in this way will ensure all team members have a role to play in the composition of the story and will (hopefully) result in a better product at the end.

Using all of this information, it is now time for students to write the first draft of the story. There are different approaches to this that your students may choose to take. Some teams will break the narrative up into parts and make team members responsible for writing different sections. Some teams will prefer to nominate a scribe, and then sit together to write the narrative as a team, contributing ideas as they come. You will need to negotiate this with your students and monitor their work to check that all team members are contributing equally.

NOTE: At some point during the create stage of the project you will want to run one or two lessons of explicit instruction relating to the mechanics of writing. My experience is that students often need greatest support with sentence structure (especially complex sentences that use a range of clause types), punctuating dialogue and using figurative language effectively to enhance descriptions. You know your students best, so it is best that we leave it to you to decide how you will develop your students' skills in these areas.

FORMATIVE ASSESSMENT

Below are some strategies you might like to use to check students' understanding and skills at this stage of the project.

- Discussions via Edmodo or a similar platform allow you to check up on student engagement and understanding.
- Make a due date for completed story plans and give feedback on these.
- At least one lesson should be devoted to peer-assessment of the draft fantasy stories.

Fantasy Story Checklist

Name

	Criteria	Peer-Assessment #1			Peer-Assessment #2		
		Didn't	Tried	Did	Didn't	Tried	Did
1	Does the story have a title?						
2	Is the climax scene fast paced? Do we think the hero might fail?						
3	Does the setting (medieval, primeval or parallel) support the narrative?						
4	Do the characters (good and bad) have believable behaviours and a back story that keeps the readers interested?						
5	Have the writers used dialogue correctly to create characters and plot?						
6	Has descriptive language been used to engage the reader's imagination, emotions and thoughts?						
7	Have the writers used correct spelling, punctuation and grammar to make sure the story is clear and easy to read?						
8	Have the writers used a variety of sentence types (simple, compound and complex) to create mood or pace?						
9	Does the story follow the traditional narrative structure appropriate to a fantasy story (sizzling start, back story, rising action, climax, resolution)						
10	Have the writers included fantastical creatures and/or a magic system (hard, middle or soft) required of the fantasy genre?						

Main strengths: (medals)

Missions: (improvements needed for this essay)

SHARE

Once students have received peer feedback on their stories and they have been refined in light of suggestions, they will need to be submitted to you for final assessment. This is an essential step for two reasons. One, you need to assess the final product to see what your students have learned and where weaknesses still exist. Two, these stories are to be published in a hard-copy collection, and students need to receive as much feedback as possible to ensure they have produced a quality story worthy of publication.

We had great success getting the Year 2 students to draw pictures of the main characters or scenes from the stories. These illustrations were then put with the completed stories in an anthology and published in a hard cover book using the online publisher Blurb, a great gift for grandparents. They have an eBook option as well. Any other publishing options are fine. Try to seek funding support from the school executive or P & C. Seeing their work printed in a 'real' book is really exciting and rewarding for students.

The second part of the 'share' stage is to Skype with the Year 2 students to read favourite excerpts from each story and to get feedback on what they enjoyed. Another great idea would be to go on an excursion to the Year 2 school so each team can give a personal story-reading to their little co-authors.

FORMATIVE ASSESSMENT

Below are some strategies you might like to use to check students' understanding and skills at this stage of the project.

- assessment of the final story using a modification of the checklist used for the drafts
- assessment of collaborative skills using a rubric or having students reflect on the contributions and effectiveness of their teammates

YEAR 10
1. EMOTIONAL EXCESS

PROJECT AT A GLANCE

 **DRIVING QUESTION:** Why do emos write poetry?

 DISCOVER: Students will conduct research into the emo subculture and the 'human condition'. They will also complete a critical study of three set poems.

 CREATE: Students will individually write an essay answering driving question and in teams they will compose a podcast addressing the driving question.

 SHARE: The completed podcasts will be presented to an audience of peers, family and an 'expert' from a local radio station or similar.

TAKE IT FURTHER: Podcasts can be shared online via iTunes U or similar.

 ASSESSMENT: The individual essay and team podcast will be assessed.

 21ST-CENTURY SKILLS: ICT, critical thinking, creative thinking, ethical understanding

LITERACY: grammar – clause structures; punctuation – layout and font; reading – making connections and visualising

MODES: listening, reading, writing and speaking

TYPE OF TEXT: informative (essay and podcast), imaginative (poetry)

LANGUAGE FEATURES OF TEXTS: allusion, evocative vocabulary, metaphor, enjambment and poetic devices

POSSIBLE TEXTS: 'Alone with Everybody' by Charles Bukowski; 'Lump' by Mark Grist; 'Still I Rise' by Maya Angelou; 'Lands End' by John Foulcher; 'All One Race' by Oodgeroo Noonuccal; 'I am Vertical' by Sylvia Plath.

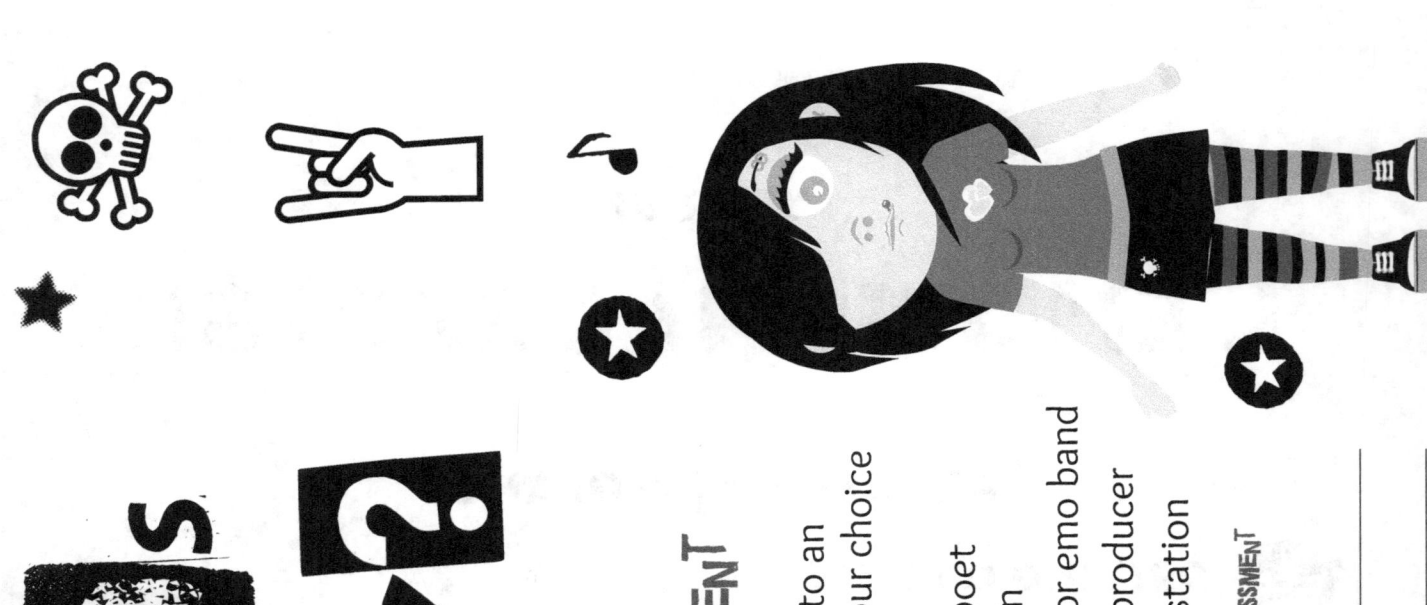

Why do Emos Write Poetry?

EXPLORE
- the poetry of three or four poets
- the similarities/differences between the poets
- the impact context has on a poet and his/her work

FORMATIVE ASSESSMENT

COMPARE
- a critical essay on two poems of your choice
- a podcast critically discussing the poetry you have studied and answering the driving question

FORMATIVE ASSESSMENT

PRESENT
- team podcast to an audience of your choice including:
  - local poet/poet organisation
  - local punk or emo band
  - radio host/producer
  - local radio station

SUMMATIVE ASSESSMENT

REPRODUCIBLE – PART TWO: SAMPLE PROJECTS YEAR 10 – 1. EMOTIONAL EXCESS

BEFORE YOU BEGIN

CONTACT EXPERTS/ROCK STARS

The strength of this project rests on the quality of the experts that you involve. Selecting an expert in advance is essential. Poetry is a difficult form for most students, however this project is designed to make connections between traditional poetry and contemporary music. This is by no means an original approach to teaching poetry, yet it is a powerful approach. Try your best to involve experts from the music industry to speak with your students about the relationship between music and poetry. Another option is to have a radio host or a producer come to critique students' podcasts. I once had Craig Schuftan (a radio producer from popular youth radio station Triple J) come and listen to my student's podcasts. His feedback was invaluable and my students still speak about his visit. You may also wish to get a poetry expert in to speak to students. This may be a local poet or an academic from a nearby university.

MODIFY PROJECT OUTLINE

A project outline has been given as a suggestion. You may like to use this outline as it is, but it is likely that you will need to modify it to match the needs of your specific students and context. Remember that PBL is all about engaging students through making content significant to their needs and interests — perhaps you will have a different driving question (what about punk or hip hop instead of emo music?) or you will add images of popular bands or musicians to make it more appealing? You will also need to modify the project outline to indicate due dates for formative and summative assessment.

ORGANISE PROJECT PACKETS

This is an important organisation strategy that we use a lot in PBL. For this project, students will be working in small teams. A project packet is essentially a small folder or document wallet given to each team that contains all of the materials essential for students to be successful with the project. These remain in the classroom and are accessed by students each lesson.

PLAN PROJECT TEAMS

Planning teams is inherently difficult, as you must consider the personality as well as the skill level of each student in your class. For this project, it is best to select a mixed team, taking into consideration the following skills: critical thinking, creativity, ICT skills and public speaking. Try to balance the teams to ensure that you have even numbers of outgoing and reserved students.

CREATE SPACE FOR A PROJECT WALL

This project wall will need to be updated regularly so students can see their understanding grow. Start your project wall with the title of the project 'Emotional Excess'. In equally large writing, put up your project's driving question — students need to see this as it will drive them through the project and inspire them to think critically. You will also need an A3 colour printout of the project outline. You may like to laminate this; we often do. Leave space for a project calendar (or put up a blank one and have a student fill it in as you negotiate due dates etc.), the 'need to know' list of questions and a good amount of space for 'key terms'. Remember that these need to be blank at the beginning of the project, as students will add this information during the 'discover' stage of learning. Use as much colour as you can, because it is important that students are attracted to it, as it is a visible record of their learning. You might even like to nominate a student to be responsible for adding new information to the 'key terms' or 'need to know' spaces.

LAUNCH YOUR PROJECT

HOOK LESSON

There are so many possibilities for how to hook your students' interest in this project. The first thing to consider is what the main conceptual focus of the project is – in this instance it could be either the emotional excess evident in poetry and emo music. If you choose punk music you might look at rebellion, or if you choose hip hop you might focus on injustice and discrimination. Another approach may focus on poetry as the most important element of the project. Finally, you might decide to focus on the type of product to be created, in this instance a podcast. Below is an outline of one way to approach the hook lesson for this project.

Have students watch a range of music videos of songs that obviously fit into the 'emo' genre or that have highly emotive lyrics and clips. Some that you might show are 'Old Scars/Future Hearts' by All Time Low, 'Can You Feel my Heart?' by Bring Me the Horizon, 'Welcome to the Black Parade' by My Chemical Romance or 'Cry' by The Used.

As students watch they can read the lyrics to the songs as well (all available online). Ask students to brainstorm as many single words to describe the songs – write these on the board. Ask students to make connections between the songs – drawing out the idea that all are highly emotive and personal. Put students in small teams and give each team the term 'emo'. Get them to complete one of the following activities:

- 5-minute brain-dump (everything they know about emo)
- 5-minute Internet research on emo
- 5-minute star bursting: who/what/when/why/where of emo
- draw pictures of an 'emo' and annotate them

Teams present these to class and explain/justify what they have included in their visual/written definitions of emo.

POSE DRIVING QUESTION

The lesson after the 'hook lesson' is very, very important. This is the lesson where students are given access to the project's driving question for the first time. This project's driving question is: *Why do emos write poetry?*

Of course, if you'd like to use another driving question, you certainly can.

Once you pose this question to the students (we often put it up on the whiteboard or the interactive whiteboard), get them to immediately write down their own, un-mediated personal response to it. This will become their 'hypothesis', which will be tested and reshaped as they work through the 'discover' learning stage.

HAND OUT PROJECT OUTLINE

We recommend that the project outline is printed off in colour or printed onto coloured paper. This sets it apart from other pieces of paper that students will receive or use during the project. The project outline is a very important document as it acts as a flyer for learning. As soon as you hand the project outline out, have students sit quietly and read through it, using a pen or highlighter to identify any information that they feel they do not understand or that they have questions about. This is an essential step, as this information becomes part of what the class has identified as what they 'need to know'. It is a good idea to encourage students to keep this project outline in their team's project packet or their own personal portfolio. We have had great success with students keeping a personal plastic sleeve folder as their 'learning portfolio'. They will use this for the entire year of projects.

ESTABLISH NEED TO KNOW

This is such an integral part of PBL. PBL is about inquiry that is led by the students. One of the best ways to begin inquiry is to ask questions. Once students have considered the driving question and have read through the project outline, they will no doubt begin to ask a lot of questions. This is a good thing. Your job is to not answer the questions, but rather encourage students to record and develop their questions further. Before you do this, take some time to get your students to focus on what they already DO know – about the project, as well as what content knowledge and skills they can bring to this project. This step is essential, as it gives you an initial understanding of where each student is at in terms of their prior knowledge – it doesn't make sense teaching content and skills they already have, does it? To support this process, we use a KWL table. Have students try to write down five things they KNOW about the project already – this will include things like knowing what they have to do (write an essay and create a podcast) and when things are due and who they are creating their products for. This information is on the project outline, but it's good to get them to transfer it to the 'What I Know' column of the KWL table so you can see that they understand the task. The next step is to get them to write down any content knowledge or skills they already have that will help them succeed with the project – this might include things like being skilled at working with audio software and an understanding of poetic devices. Make sure you go around and see what each student has written, this will help you know where and how to distribute your time during the project.

Now it's time to start recording those questions. You may like to do this as a class group – having students call out their questions and allocating one student the role of scribe. These questions can then be recorded onto the project wall, becoming a guide for students' learning through the project. If you think students need to develop their questioning strategies, you could try using the star-bursting technique. Have students draw a six-pointed star in the middle of a sheet of paper. On each point write: where, what, how, when, why, which. Encourage students to think of as many questions about the project (and its related content) beginning with each word, and record them on their paper. You will be surprised by the richness and diversity of the questions students ask.

CREATE A PROJECT CALENDAR

A project calendar is designed to keep students forward-focused. PBL is a student-directed methodology, where students are required to take responsibility for their own learning. As such, a project calendar can help students keep themselves organised and ensure that they are working toward clearly established deadlines. These deadlines should be negotiated with the teacher as a whole class. However, there will be times when individual teams will have different deadlines to ensure that learning is differentiated effectively. We recommend that a project calendar includes clearly identified dates for formative assessment, that is assessment of learning through strategies like plans, drafts, mini-presentations, quizzes and meetings with team leaders. This project has students completing two products – an essay and a podcast. The project calendar must reflect opportunities for teams to receive feedback on these products at the process stage. Students will also negotiate opportunities for direct instruction with the teacher – this is where the teacher runs a traditional, teacher-centred lesson.

EMO

- Desires comfort and security
- Passionate emotions about themselves or others
- Negative, depressed outlook on life
- Unhappiness stems from negative life experiences
- Desires to be seen as being different or apart from mainstream society

DISCOVER

The first thing to do with this project is to check students' prior knowledge about poetry. There are two possibilities for this:

1. In teams, students are to create a 'picture of poetry' (words and images; colourful) that is annotated with everything they know about poetry. These are stuck up on the class walls for the class to see.
2. Edmodo quiz (or paper quiz) of poetic terms. Students can keep taking the test until they get 100% – mastery learning. This is a strategy used in PBL and encourages students to learn from their mistakes and to keep trying.

A significant amount of the discover cycle of learning for this project will be teacher-driven. You may use the strategy outlined below, or you may have your own preferred method for modelling how to critically engage with poetry.

- Select a poem to use as a model for the class. Tell the class that you are modelling the process of critical analysis. Ask them, 'Why do you need to know this?' They should be able to say, 'Because we have to write a critical essay and make a podcast.'
- Read the poem to the class. Pose the questions: What is the poem about? Why was the poem written? Demonstrate how you use the 'what I know' and 'what I wonder' thinking strategy as you go through the poem – write these on the board.
- Use a KWL table to support this and to encourage critical thinking. Model this by writing two or three things that you feel confident you know about the poem. Now write two or three 'what I wonder' questions in the W column, e.g. 'I wonder why the poet used this metaphor?' or 'I wonder why the poem is structured in this way?' Give students an opportunity to try and answer your 'what I wonder' questions. Together, come to a consensus on why the poem was written and what the poet is saying.
- Now identify some powerful techniques used to convey this meaning – this is the HOW. Just select about four or five – enough to write two great paragraphs. On the board, use the information you have gathered through your analysis to write two analytical paragraphs about the poem. This is NOT meant to be a really detailed analysis of a poem – just a quick lesson on how to do it. This can be quite an intimidating task to perform in front of the class, so you might want to prepare your analysis before the lesson so you feel more confident. These paragraphs will act as a model for what students need to produce themselves: a critical essay. Have students highlight key elements of analysis evident in the sample paragraphs.
- Lead a class discussion about what makes a good or bad essay. Focus on language and sentence structure – what makes a sophisticated sentence? Co-construct a rubric for essay writing – with levels ranging from 'great' to 'awful'. The 'great' criteria become the checklist for student essays. You should also take some this time to focus on the necessary features of an introduction and a conclusion.
- Allocate each team a different poem. Encourage students to annotate their poems with abstract nouns summarising ideas/mood of each line or stanza, highlight obvious and effective techniques and use a paragraph scaffold once they are ready to write – see resource provided. Make sure you take time to work with individual students/teams where help is needed. Encourage students to do some research into personal, social, cultural and historical factors that influenced the writing of the poem – this will help them to more fully answer the driving question. Request that each team presents a PowerPoint summary of the poem and their analysis to the class.

FORMATIVE ASSESSMENT

This project calls for some serious formative assessment strategies. We like to use end-of-lesson reflections using the 'medals and missions' strategy – this sees students identifying one thing that lesson that they mastered and one thing that they still need to master relating to the project. This is a simple but effective way of having students reflect on their learning.

We also love to use Post-It notes for formative assessment.

Try this activity:

- At the end of the lesson, give each student two Post-It notes (two different colours) and ask them to write one thing they learnt about the poet/poem that lesson and one thing they are still puzzled by. Names need to go on the Post-Its. Teacher uses these to determine whom to help the next lesson.

POETRY QUIZ

Read through the lines of poetry below and identify the poetic device(s) being used.

1. I sneezed a sneeze into the air,
It fell to earth I know not where.
Poetic device: _____

2. It goes fwunkety,
then slunkety,
as the washing goes around.
Poetic device: _____

3. The sea has a laugh
And the cliff a frown;
For the laugh of the sea
Is wearing him down.
Poetic device: _____

4. Half a league, half a league,
Half a league onward,
All in the valley of Death
Rode the six hundred.
Poetic device: _____

5. And on a day we meet to walk the line
And set the wall between us once again.
We keep the wall between us as we go.
Poetic device: _____

6. The sea is a hungry dog,
Giant and grey.
Poetic device: _____

7. The drivers are washing the concrete mixers;
Like elephant tenders they hose them down.
Poetic device: _____

8. On either side of the river lie
Long fields of barley and of rye,
That clothe the wold and meet the sky.
Poetic device: _____

9. By channels of coolness the echoes are calling,
And down the dim gorges I hear the creek falling.
Poetic device: _____

REPRODUCIBLE – PART TWO: SAMPLE PROJECTS YEAR 10 – 1. EMOTIONAL EXCESS

90

POETRY ANALYSIS TABLE

WHAT IDEA IS THE FOCUS OF THIS PARAGRAPH?	WHAT TECHNIQUE IS BEING USED TO SAY THIS IN THE POEM?	WHAT IS AN EXAMPLE OF THIS TECHNIQUE BEING USED?	WHAT DOES THIS TECHNIQUE MAKE YOU THINK, FEEL OR IMAGINE RELATING TO THE FOCUS IDEA?	WHY IS THIS IDEA IMPORTANT TO PEOPLE IN THE WORLD? RESTATE THE MAIN IDEA OF THE PARAGRAPH

REPRODUCIBLE – PART TWO: SAMPLE PROJECTS YEAR 10 – 1. EMOTIONAL EXCESS

CREATE 🎵

It is now time for the students to decide which two poems they would like to focus on for their essay answering the driving question. Remind them that this part of the project is paramount to creating an effective podcast. Individually, students are to begin drafting their essay. The essay is an individual task, however students should still spend time with their team in class. Students will use their teammates as critical friends to receive feedback and feed-forward on their draft essays. This process is supported by an essay checklist based on the 'great' criteria that the class devised in earlier lessons. A blank checklist is in 'Part Three: Additional Resources'. Students should receive feedback and feed-forward from TWO peers. It is a good idea for the teacher to model how to use the checklist, how to annotate a draft and how to give 'medals and missions' feedback/feed-forward. There is information on this process in Part One: The What, the Why and the How of Project Based Learning on pages 14–16. There is also a template for you to create your own checklist.

Give students an opportunity to spend a few minutes looking at their project calendar to see what goals have been met and what needs to be changed. They will likely identify that it is time to begin work on their podcast. This process of reflection on learning helps students to celebrate their hard work. Learning is hard.

In teams, students negotiate roles and responsibilities for the podcast product. Teams will need to decide which TWO poems will be the focus of the podcast. Students will then need to complete a mini inquiry into the language, forms and features of a podcast – however, this should only take one or two lessons and can be achieved primarily by listening to some podcasts online. Some great, now-defunct examples are the Poetica podcasts from ABC Radio National or the Culture Club podcasts by Triple J's Craig Schuftan:

www..abc.net.au/radionational/programs/poetica/

craigschuftan.com/radio-series/

Students will work as a team to plan and script their podcast. You should work with individual teams to guide them through the process; don't worry if you don't know how to create a podcast, just relax and learn with your students. The podcasts only need to be a maximum of three minutes in length. Urge them to include sound effects and music clips to make their podcasts engaging.

FORMATIVE ASSESSMENT

Below are some strategies you might like to use to check students' understanding and skills at this stage of the project. These are typically tasks completed in the last 5–10 minutes of a lesson:

- Give each student two different-coloured pieces of paper about the size of a postcard. On one piece, students write something they feel they can confidently teach their peers relating to the product (essay) or the driving question. On the other piece, students write something they would like help with relating to the product (essay) or the driving question. These are put into separate boxes for the next lesson.
- 30-second share – each student stands up and shares one thing they have discovered about poetry/a poet/the driving question/essay-writing. Encourage students to share original ideas and avoid repeating what other students have already shared. Celebrate learning with some type of reward.

- On a piece of paper, students are to identify who they think is working the most and the least in their team.
- Each team presents 'Five Things You Need to Know about Podcasts' to the class. These form loose criteria for the podcast – teacher can add extra criteria where necessary (e.g. quotes from poems or eminent poetry critics).

MARKING CRITERIA

CRITERIA \ LEVEL	SKILFUL 5	EFFECTIVE 4	SOUND 3	LIMITED 2	ELEMENTARY 1
FOCUSES ON THE CONCEPTS IMPLIED IN THE DRIVING QUESTION (POETRY, HUMAN CONDITION, EMO)	Highly developed, complex and personal response to the driving question outlined in introduction and developed in body of essay.	Well-developed, thoughtful and personal response to the driving question outlined in introduction and developed in body of essay.	Sound response to the driving question outlined in introduction and somewhat developed in body of essay.	Limited response to the driving question outlined in introduction and poorly developed in body of essay.	Required elements are missing or incomplete
UNDERSTANDS HOW COMPOSERS USE FEATURES OF TEXTS	Skilful use of the analytical paragraph structure to demonstrate a sophisticated understanding of how composers use features of texts to express their emotions and ideas about the human condition	Effective use of analytical paragraph structure to demonstrate a well-developed understanding of how composers use features of texts to express their emotions and ideas about the human condition	Sound use of analytical paragraph structure to demonstrate an understanding of how composers use features of texts to express their emotions and ideas about the human condition	Attempts to use elements of analytical paragraph structure to demonstrate a developing understanding of how composers use features of texts to express their emotions and ideas about the human condition	Required elements are missing or incomplete
COMPOSES A SUSTAINED ARGUMENT SUPPORTED BY TEXTUAL EVIDENCE	Composes a sophisticated, logical and sustained argument supported by detailed and relevant textual evidence	Composes a logical and sustained argument supported by detailed textual evidence	Composes an argument supported by textual evidence	Attempts to compose an argument supported by some textual evidence	Required elements are missing or incomplete
USES LANGUAGE AND STRUCTURE OF AN ESSAY	Skilful control of the language and structure of an essay — beginning each paragraph with a well-selected conceptual noun. Few or no errors.	Effective control of the language and structure of an essay — begins most paragraphs with conceptual nouns. Few errors.	Sound control of the language and structure of an essay — some paragraphs begin with conceptual noun. Some errors.	Attempts to use the language and structure of an essay — fails to use conceptual nouns. Includes frequent errors	Required elements are missing or incomplete

EMOS ESSAY SELF AND PEER ASSESSMENT

NAME: _____ TEACHER: _____

CRITERIA (GOALS)	SELF-ASSESSMENT			PEER ASSESSMENT		
	I DIDN'T	I TRIED TO	I DID	DIDN'T	TRIED TO	DID
Did you/your peer demonstrate a strong understanding of poetry, the human condition and what it means to be classified 'emo'?						
Did you/your peer clearly outline your argument in response to the driving question in the introduction?						
Did you/your peer relate each of your arguments to the driving question?						
Did you name your/your peer's texts and the composers in the introduction?						
Did your/your peer's lines of argument build to a logical conclusion (showing cause and effect between ideas)?						
Did you/your peer give enough evidence (quotes or descriptions) for each of your arguments? (12 quotes)						
Did you/your peer use the STEEL paragraph structure for each paragraph?						
Did you/your peer start each paragraph with a strong conceptual noun or noun phrase? (nominalisation)						
Did you/your peer use correct punctuation and spelling?						
MAIN STRENGTHS (MEDALS)						
IMPROVEMENTS NEEDED FOR THIS ESSAY (MISSIONS)						

REPRODUCIBLE – PART TWO: SAMPLE PROJECTS YEAR 10 – 1. EMOTIONAL EXCESS

SHARE

PRESENTATION OF PODCASTS

Rehearsing is so important at this stage. No one wants to listen to a boring or badly recorded podcast. Students should work as a team to rehearse and record their podcast. Work with individual teams to guide them through the process. The quality of sound is really important, so make sure you allow enough time for students to experiment with the audio-recording software they have chosen to use. This will ensure a better quality product. If you don't have laptops or tablets, this will require access to a computer room. If this is the case, make sure you book this well in advance.

Students should take time to prepare for the presentation of podcasts to invited guests. Ensure each team rehearses their speech and checks that their podcast is ready to be heard. The presentation can occur in school time, in the library or a similar space. Organise a student to open the event with a brief overview of the project they've been doing and have them introduce your guests. Your guests might like to speak briefly about their experiences with poetry, music and podcasts.

SUMMATIVE ASSESSMENT

Below are some strategies you might like to use to check students' understanding and skills at this stage of the project.

- Have students complete the 'L' column of the KWL table they were working on at the beginning of the project
- Use class-created criteria for presentation and peer assessment of podcasts

POST-PROJECT REFLECTION/EVALUATION

After the presentation of the podcasts, have a celebration of project success lesson with lollies or chips and music. Use the beginning of that lesson to have students evaluate the project and their learning by completing the 'Emo Project Reflection' questions.

EMO PROJECT REFLECTION

1. One of the learning goals of this project was to be able to write an analytical essay. How well did you achieve this goal?

2. During this project you engaged with some complex poetry. Which poem did you find the most challenging? Why?

3. What ICT skills did you develop as a result of creating a podcast with your team?

4. What is something that was hard for you at the start of the project, but easy now?

5. This project aimed to develop your appreciation for why people write poetry. How has your appreciation of poetry developed?

6. What in our class has made the biggest impact on your learning during this project? Why?

7. What is something the teacher could have done to make this project better?

8. If you could turn back time and do this project again, what would you do differently?

REPRODUCIBLE – PART TWO: SAMPLE PROJECTS YEAR 10 – 1. EMOTIONAL EXCESS

YEAR 10

2. MORE THAN MEETS THE EYE

PROJECT AT A GLANCE

 **DRIVING QUESTION:** What makes a story worth stealing?

 DISCOVER: Students will read and analyse a prescribed novel. In a small team, students will write a literary essay comparing the novel to its appropriation – a film or video game. Students will research fan-fiction genres and conventions.

 CREATE: As an individual, students will compose a fan-fiction story based on their favourite text.

 SHARE: Students' fan-fiction stories will be published online at fanfiction.com. Students will also organise an event to launch and sell a collection of their fan-fiction stories which will be published using Blurb. The money raised from this event will be donated to a literacy-related charity.

 ASSESSMENT: The literary essay and the fan-fiction story will be assessed.

 21ST-CENTURY SKILLS: critical thinking, creative thinking and collaboration

LITERACY: grammar – clause structures, sentence types, voice; reading – questioning, summarising and making connections

MODES: reading, writing and viewing

TYPE OF TEXT: informative (literary essay) and imaginative (fan fiction)

LANGUAGE FEATURES OF TEXTS: theme, plot, characterisation, settings, figurative language, film/visual techniques and motif

POSSIBLE TEXTS: *Harry Potter*; *Hunger Games*; *Divergent*; *The Fault in Our Stars*; *1984*; *Tomorrow When the War Began*; *Girl with the Dragon Tattoo*.

WHAT MAKES A STORY WORTH STEALING?

STEAL

Respond to an original text and its appropriation in order to steal their transformation tricks.

MOD

Through a process of planning, drafting and editing, compose a 1000–2000 word piece of fan fiction that transforms one of your favourite stories.

PEDDLE

Read aloud: select your favourite passage from your story and read it to your peers.

Share your story with a wider readership by publishing it on the fan-fiction site or Wattpad.

BEFORE YOU BEGIN

CONTACT EXPERTS/ROCK STARS

Fan fiction is VERY popular online. You would be surprised by how many of your students read it for pleasure, and even more surprised by how many write it in their spare time. The prevalence of fan fiction and fan-fiction writers means that it should be relatively easy to get in contact with a fan-fiction writer. You may have ex-students who are fan-fiction writers, so it's worth reaching out to that part of your network and asking. It would be ideal if you could organise a writer to come and speak to students just before they begin to plan their own fan fiction and then return for the book launch fund-raiser.

MODIFY PROJECT OUTLINE

Now is the time to modify the given project outline. You may decide to change some of the key elements in order to meet the needs of your students. Look closely at the three stages of learning – discover, create, share – and consider what might need to be modified. Remember that PBL is all about engaging students through making content significant for their needs and interests. You will also need to modify the project outline to indicate due dates for formative and summative assessment.

ORGANISE PROJECT PACKETS

This is a rather complex project, as it requires that students develop their understanding of appropriation/adaptation/transformation, engage with two texts and then write their own fan fiction. To help keep your students' learning on track and to keep them organised, use your project packets well. There are a number of resources that will be useful to include in these project packets, including:

- Information on structure and language of comparison essay. These resources should match the needs of your students and may take the form of worksheets or links to websites with interactive activities. Some students will require scaffolds to support their writing.
- Information on fan fiction. As with the above, this may simply take the form of a worksheet students complete using information from their own inquiry, or you may choose to give them specific information. This choice will depend on the skills of your students and your ability to access technology.
- Team contract (you might like to use the one provided in Part 3: Additional Resources)
- Checklist for comparison essay
- Checklist for fan fiction
- Project calendar
- Copy of project outline

PLAN PROJECT TEAMS

This is a project where you might like to 'stream' your teams into ability groups. This will allow you to spend more time working closely with the teams of students who require much more support to be successful with the project.

We would suggest teams be no bigger than four. This will give each student the potential to contribute meaningfully to this project.

CREATE SPACE FOR A PROJECT WALL

Your project wall needs to be highly visible. If you don't have a home-room, you might like to seek permission from the school executive to use an external space, such as a wall outside of a classroom that you use for that class. Another alternative is to have a digital project wall. There are some great web tools to create these, such as Weebly and Glogster. These sites allow you to create interactive project walls, where students can click on the project outline and see it in greater detail, or access additional resources like scaffolds or checklists. Things to include on this project's wall:

- project outline
- project calendar
- key terms
- need to know
- project title
- project's driving question.

LAUNCH YOUR PROJECT

HOOK LESSON

As with all projects, the hook lesson must be fun and engaging for students and launch inquiry into the project's content. This project provides you with a range of options to engage your students. Here is one suggestion for a fun hook lesson.

- Read students a 'fractured fairytale' and ask them what is familiar and what is unfamiliar.
- In teams, have students compete to generate the longest list of 'transformed' texts — novels, films, video games. The team with the longest list wins a chocolate.

POSE DRIVING QUESTION

The lesson after the 'hook lesson' is where students are given access to the project's driving question for the first time. This project's driving question is: **What makes a story worth stealing?** This is an example of a short, snappy driving question that should easily engage students. The content is familiar to them because they are accustomed to stories being reworked and re-imagined as games, films and television shows.

Of course, if you don't like this question, or you think your students won't, you can change it to something more suitable. Once you pose this question to the students, get them to immediately write down their own, unmediated personal response to it. This will become their 'hypothesis', which will be tested and reshaped as they work through the 'discover' learning stage.

HAND OUT PROJECT OUTLINE

We recommend that the project outline is printed off in colour or printed onto coloured paper. As soon as you hand the project outline out, have students sit quietly and read through it, using a pen or highlighter to identify any information that they feel they do not understand or that they have questions about. This is an essential step, as this information becomes part of what the class has identified as what they 'need to know'.

ESTABLISH NEED TO KNOW

This is your opportunity to have students share all of their questions about the project. What you want from your students is to begin asking open-ended and critical questions that acknowledge that more learning must occur and that the teacher does not know everything. You can make establishing the need-to-know questions into a game. Have all students write down questions that they feel they need to know the answers to in order to be successful. Tell them that in order to win this game, the originality and quality of the questions is very important. Ask all students to stand behind their desks. Have each student read out one of their questions. If others have the same question and do not have any other original questions, they must sit down. Keep going around the room, having students contribute their questions until there is only one person left standing. As the questions are being read out, write the really good ones on the board to create a class list of what they 'need to know' to complete the project successfully.

SET UP TEAMS

Putting students into their teams is usually a noisy activity. A good way to get them to stay quiet is to write the names of the team members on the board and then tell the class that those who find their team members the quickest while remaining silent will get a prize. At this stage it is a good idea to tell students that they will be working with their teams closely during the 'discovery' stage of the project to complete inquiry activities such as writing the comparative essay, however they will be composing their fan fictions individually. It is up to you if you wish to draw attention to or deflect attention from the fact that the teams have been chosen based on ability.

CREATE A PROJECT CALENDAR

A project calendar is designed to keep students forward-focused. PBL is a student-directed methodology where students are required to take responsibility for their own learning. As such, a project calendar can help students keep themselves organised and ensure that they are working toward clearly established deadlines. Some things to include on the project calendar for this project are:

- due dates for essay plan, draft and revised version
- due dates for fan-fiction plan, draft and revised version
- date of fund-raiser.

DISCOVER

The discovery stage for this project is quite teacher-directed. It is not teacher-centred, however, as students are actively working through a range of collaborative learning tasks to develop their understanding of the ways in which stories can be appropriated, adapted and transformed. The following is a suggested series of activities you may wish to run with your students at this stage of the project.

- Have students research the personal, historical, cultural and social context of the composers of your two texts. This is important, as they will be considering how context impacts the form, style and ideas of a text.

- Introduce the Five Elements of Narrative using the Fractured Fairytale used in the hook lesson. Explain that these elements will be the focus of student responses to the texts, as this will help them prepare for their own creative compositions.

- Students begin responding to the first text. As they respond, students are to complete a 'where/why lotus diagram' to track their understanding of Five Elements of Narrative. To make this more manageable for students, teachers can use the 'jigsaw' strategy. Where you might like to number students 1, 2, 3, 4 — with each number responsible for a specific section of the lotus. After viewing, students must then team up with peers with different numbers to access their notes and complete the lotus. An alternative is to have each team be in charge of an 'element'. This strategy can continue until the text is finished.

- Introduce Bloom's Revised Taxonomy, focusing students on the VERBS relevant to each section of the taxonomy. Explain that questions are driven by these verbs and show examples. Explain the difference between the four main verbs: define, describe, explain and analyse. Uses the Example Questions handout to model how to respond to questions using each of the four main verbs. The 'analyse' question should use an analytical paragraph structure — define, describe, explain, evaluate. These will be the focus of the short-answer questions students will complete based on the first text.

- Students are given the Responding to Prescribed Text short-answer questions. Students think/pair/share their responses to the questions. Encourage students to work in their teams to use their notes on lotus diagrams to help with their answers to the questions.

- Students begin responding to the second text. As they respond, students are to complete the 'where/why lotus diagram' to track their understanding of Five Elements of Narrative. They should use the same process for sharing notes as used with the first text. This strategy continues until the text is finished.

- Hand out the 'Responding to Prescribed Text' short-answer questions — these are based on the second prescribed text. Students think/pair/share their responses to the questions. Once again, encourage students to use their notes on the lotus diagram to help with their answers to the questions.

- Divide students into 'discovery teams' of five students. Each student in a team is assigned a narrative element to become an 'expert' in. Experts are to individually complete the THREE questions on the 'Element Expert' handout, and then they are to join with their fellow experts to share their ideas and, as an expert team, complete the last question on the 'Element Expert' handout. Experts then return to their 'discovery' team and share their expertise with their peers. By the end of this activity, all students should have one paragraph on each narrative element with examples from both texts studied.

- As a class, discuss the similarities and differences between the original text and its appropriation. Prompt them to give reasons why they think these changes were made in light of the context and form of both texts.

FORMATIVE ASSESSMENT

Below are some strategies you might like to use to check students' understanding and skills at this stage of the project.

- Teacher to check completed lotus diagrams to ensure all students are engaged and understanding the content
- Collaborative behaviours can be assessed using a rubric or checklist (see Part Three: Additional Resources for examples)

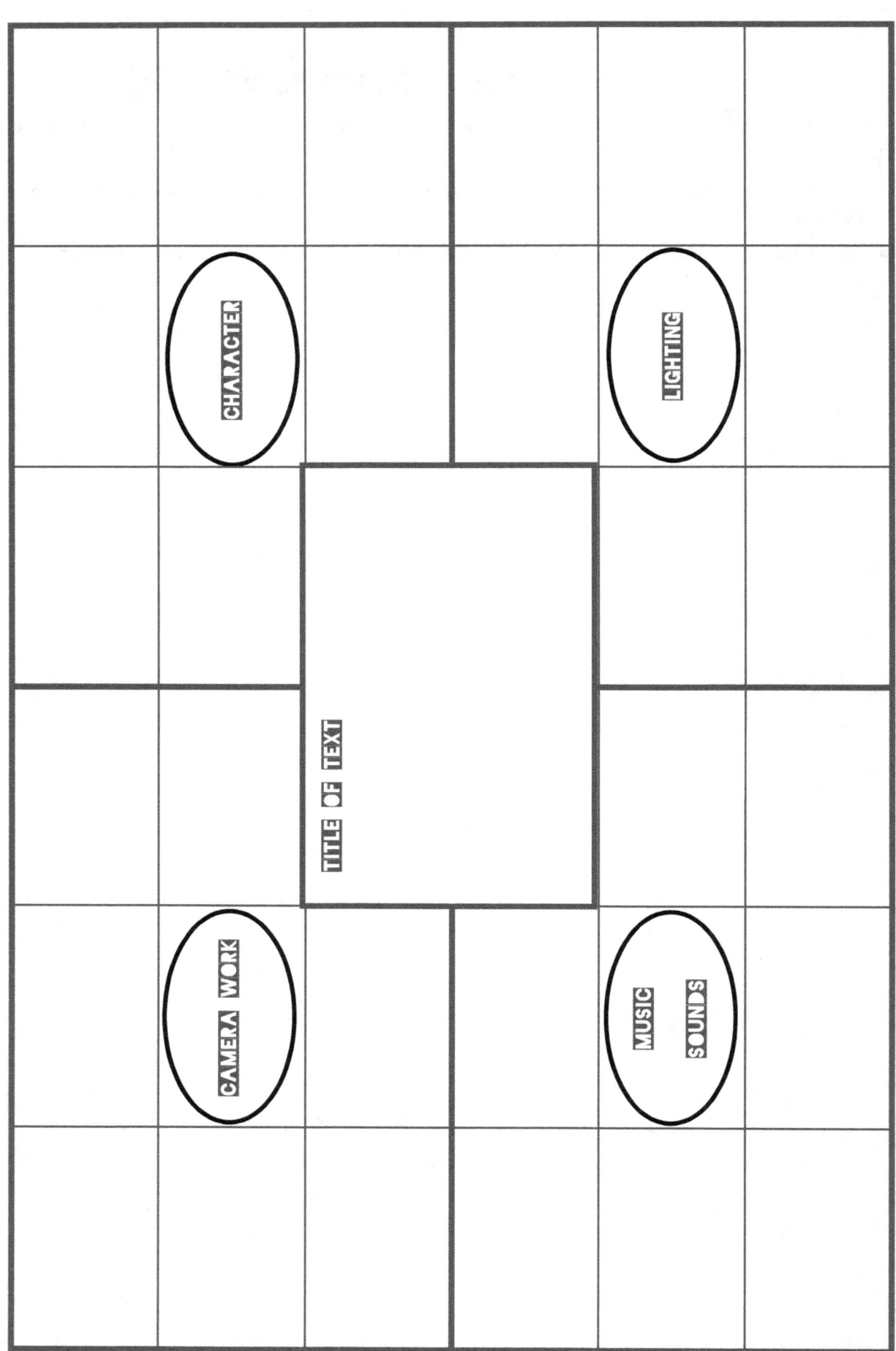

REPRODUCIBLE – PART TWO: SAMPLE PROJECTS YEAR 10 – 2. MORE THAN MEETS THE EYE

BLOOM'S REVISED TAXONOMY

TO DEMONSTRATE:	TAXONOMY	USEFUL VERBS
LOWER-ORDER THINKING SKILLS (LOTS)	REMEMBERING	List; describe; find; state; name; identify
	UNDERSTANDING	Explain; interpret; distinguish; relate; translate; compare; describe
	APPLYING	Solve; show; use; illustrate; calculate; construct; complete; examine; outline
HIGHER-ORDER THINKING SKILLS (HOTS)	ANALYSING	Analyse; distinguish; examine; compare; contrast; investigate; categorise; identify; explain; separate; advertise
	EVALUATING	Judge; select; choose; decide; justify; debate; verify; argue; recommend; assess; discuss; rate; prioritise; compare
	CREATING	Create, Invent, Compose, Predict, Plan, Construct, Design, Imagine, Propose, Devise, Formulate, Combine, Hypothesise

EXAMPLE QUESTIONS FOR EACH LEVEL OF THINKING

1. What is a simile?
2. Describe the behaviour of Macbeth when the witches tell him he will be king.
3. Identify an example of descriptive language in the passage.
4. Explain why Juliet refuses to marry Paris.
5. Describe the mood of the poem.
6. Outline the ways in which the events in *A Property of the Clan* reflect the behaviour of teenagers today.
7. Compare how the poets you have studied represent the theme of 'loss' in their poems.
8. In your view, which TWO of these texts most effectively explore how feelings of belonging and not belonging may shift with time?

TASK: FOR EACH QUESTION, HIGHLIGHT THE KEY VERB THAT INDICATES WHAT TYPE OF ANSWER IS REQUIRED

FOUR TYPES OF ENGLISH QUESTIONS

For this project, you should be able to answer the four types of questions below. These questions and answers are based on the photograph. Pay attention to the sample answers, especially the content and their length.

1. Describe the photograph. (Remembering)

   The photograph is a close-up of a small child with large, sad-looking eyes holding his hands to his head and sitting at the bottom of a staircase.

2. Explain what the eyes reveal about the child's emotions. (Understanding)

   The large, dark eyes of the small child reveal that he is unhappy or anxious because they are opened wide, yet look dark and heavy. One eye is hidden by the boy's right arm, but the visible eye stares out at us, sadly, and clearly suggests that his mood is dark.

3. Discuss how the hands shape your response to the child. (Analysing)

   The placement of the boy's hands seems to suggest that something terrible has just happened, and serve to heighten the expression on the boy's face. His posture indicates that he is reacting to something horrible, as it seems defensive and like he is subconsciously curling up to protect himself. All these factors engender a sense of sympathy for the child, and we wonder what he has just run away from and whether it is coming down the stairs after him.

4. How effectively does this image capture the photographer's sympathy for the child? (Evaluating)

   The photographer uses dark shadows, layout and gaze to effectively capture the sympathy he has for the child. The photo creates a sombre mood, reflective of the child's mood which is revealed through his gaze, expression and posture. Everything, from the framing and the use of shadowy background to the stance of the boy and his pitiful expression, effectively forces the viewer to wonder what has caused his distress. The photographer seems to feel sympathy for the small child who is clearly unhappy, and the stairs leading away from him seem to suggest that what he is unhappy about is just around the corner.

RESPONDING TO PRESCRIBED TEXT

Base your answers to the questions below on the text you have studied in class. Remember to pay attention to the types of VERBS used in each question.

1. Identify the main characters and settings in the text.

   ....
   ....
   ....

2. Describe the plot of your text.

   ....
   ....
   ....

3. Explain the main theme of your text.

   ....
   ....
   ....

4. Analyse how the composer has used one element of narrative to communicate his/her main theme.

   ....
   ....
   ....

ELEMENT EXPERT

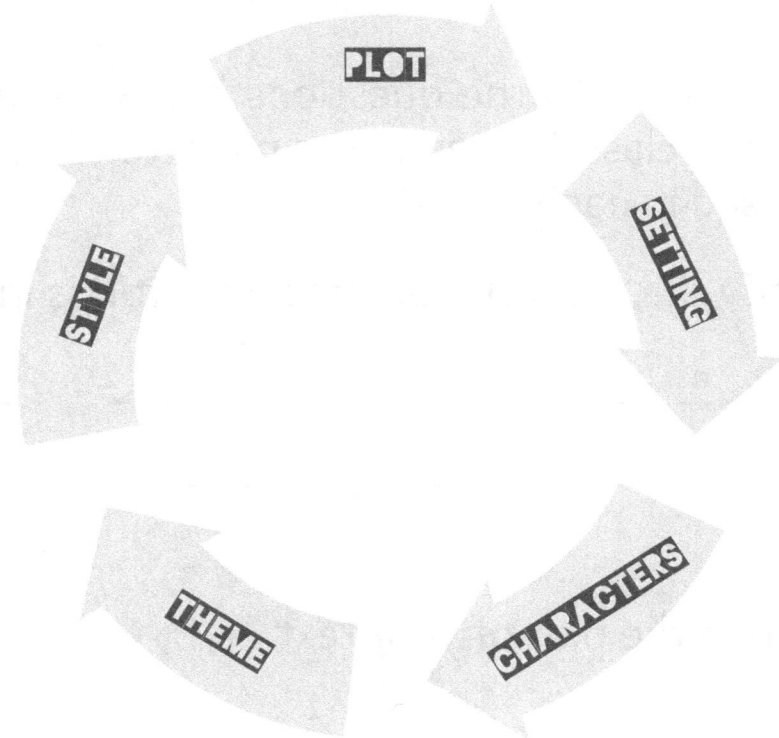

1. Identify FOUR quotes/scenes/openings that provide information about characters/setting/plot/theme/style – two from each text.

2. Explain why you think the composer has included this quote/scene/opening.

3. Discuss how the composer has used this character/setting/plot/theme/style to engage their responders.

4. Evaluate which composer has used their characters/setting/plot/theme/style more effectively.

CREATE 🎵

There are two products that students will be creating in this project — the team comparative essay and the individual fan fiction. In the discover stage of the project, students developed their understanding of how and why stories are appropriate, adapted or transformed. To fully demonstrate their understanding, each team will work together to use their notes and their research on context to write a comparative essay. This will provide you with a chance to discuss the language features of essays, especially sentence structure focusing on the use of nominalisations and connectives.

Remind students about the following conventions of naming texts in formal essays.

- Once the final essays have been submitted to you for assessment, ask students to return to the project outline to check their progress. At this point the class will check which **NEED TO KNOW** questions they have answers to and record these in their workbooks. They will then focus on the questions they are yet to answer — it is likely that these will be related to the fan-fiction task.

- Teacher refocuses students on the 'compose' stage of learning. Students complete the 'individual task planner' to help them direct their learning for the remainder of the project. They must allocate time for planning, drafting, seeking peer/teacher feedback and editing.

- An opportunity exists at this point to spend a lesson or two focusing on fan fiction as a form. You may wish to lead this learning, or you may wish to set your students the task of researching on the Internet. Be warned, there are some racy fan-fiction stories available, so be sure to let your students know to use their judgment well when accessing resources online.

- Students select an original text to base their stories on and then begin planning their story. They can use the 'Fan-fiction Planner' document supplied. Encourage students to seek teacher feedback on their plans before they begin to write their drafts. Students will need approximately one week to write their first draft and then seek peer or teacher feedback to refine it. It is preferable that team members assess each others' stories, acting as 'beta writers', as this is what happens in the online fan-fiction communities.

FORMATIVE ASSESSMENT

Below are some strategies you might like to use to check students' understanding and skills at this stage of the project.

- peer feedback on comparative essay using checklist
- students use a 'Narrative Checklist' to self-assess their draft and refine
- refined drafts are given to two peers for feedback using the **MEDALS and MISSIONS** protocol and a 'Narrative Checklist'
- students use the feedback from their peers to edit and refine their stories, and this version is submitted to the teacher for final feedback.

PROJECT MANAGEMENT LOG: INDIVIDUAL GUIDE

DRIVING QUESTION: _____

NAME: _____

TASK	DUE DATE	STATUS	DONE

This document reproduced with permission from BIE

REPRODUCIBLE — PART TWO: SAMPLE PROJECTS YEAR 10 — 2. MORE THAN MEETS THE EYE

SHARE

When students have finalised their stories, devote a lesson to students reading out their favourite passages to their peers. This is an enjoyable activity but also helps you choose which students will read excerpts at the Fan-Fiction Fund-raiser.

When planning for the fund-raiser, have students organise and set up the venue. This will include setting up chairs, organising microphones, planning who will bring refreshments and ensuring copies of the collected stories are ready to be sold. The collection of stories would look best bound with a colour cover. You can organise this to be done at school or through an online publisher. You may need to ask the school executive to help pay for this, or the P&C could as a donation. One idea is that guests pay around $10 or $15 admission to the event, and receive a copy of the book plus refreshments, as well as getting to hear an author speak about fan fiction. Having students read excerpts from their stories and talk about the project is a nice touch. All money raised from the event should be donated to a literacy-related charity such as the Indigenous Literacy Foundation.

Additionally, students should upload their stories to fan fiction websites such as *www.wattpad.com* or *www.fanfiction.net*.

YEAR 10
3. SOMETHING WICKED

PROJECT AT A GLANCE

 **DRIVING QUESTION:** How can we design a winning advertising campaign for a production of *Macbeth*?

 DISCOVER: With the class, students read the play *Macbeth*. They also discover the art of advertising, specifically theatre advertising and the design process.

 CREATE: Students will work in teams to create an advertising campaign and pitch for a production of *Macbeth*.

 SHARE: Students will pitch their campaign to a Shakespeare and/or advertising expert.

 ASSESSMENT: Students will be assessed on their team's advertising campaign and pitch.

 21ST-CENTURY SKILLS: ethical understanding, ICT, collaboration, critical thinking and communication

LITERACY: grammar – clause combinations, technicality and abstractions; spelling – nominalisations; punctuation – layout and font; reading – monitoring and making connections

MODES: reading (play), viewing and representing/creating (advertisement)

TYPE OF TEXTS: persuasive (advertising campaign) and imaginative (play)

LANGUAGE FEATURES OF TEXTS: iambic pentameter, blank verse, soliloquy, aside, embedded stage directions, apostrophe, allusions

POSSIBLE TEXTS: Shakespeare's *Macbeth*; *No Fear Shakespeare: Macbeth*; Roman Polanski's *Macbeth*; *Throne of Blood* by Akira Kurosawa; Justin Kurzel's *Macbeth*; Orson Welles' *Macbeth*.

How can we design a winning advertising campaign for a production of Macbeth?

Inquire

- Familiarise yourself with the play *Macbeth* by William Shakespeare. Find out about the plot, characters, themes and the use of imagery and symbols in *Macbeth*.
- Find out about advertising creative work.
- Find out the needs and wants of your given theatre audience.

Assessment for lesson

- quiz
- team presentation

Design

- Use the design thinking process to design your team's advertising campaign.
- Create polished advertisements to show during your 'pitch'.

Assessment for lesson

- draft advertisements

Pitch

- Write a draft design pitch.
- Refine your design pitch using feedback.
- Deliver a polished design concept pitch to a Shakespeare/advertising expert. Compete to win.

Assessment for lesson

- pitch and final advertisements

Three Witches Theatre Co.

Attention: Young Design Teams

The Challenge

Three Witches Theatre Company is seeking a young design team to help promote its upcoming production of William Shakespeare's *Macbeth*. Does your design team have what it takes to be THE team behind this campaign? To be in contention for the contract, each member of your team must submit a design proposal for ONE print advertisement for the company's production of *Macbeth*. The theatre company expects the team to develop a strong idea and theme that runs through the campaign.

Target Audience

The theatre company has decided that the winning design will determine the direction of their production of *Macbeth*. This means that you and your design team can choose who the target audience will be for the production. It is essential that the target audience is decided upon BEFORE your team begins designing the campaign.

Considerations

- The play *Macbeth* raises many ideas and themes. The director has indicated that the design team may choose to focus the advertising campaign on any idea or theme they feel is the most central or powerful in the play.
- The campaign will be highly visible and therefore should incorporate a range of media channels – e.g. billboards, posters, postcards, website ads, magazine ads, bus ads. The design team must negotiate who will be responsible for each media channel.

Mandatory Requirements

While our director is giving you full creative licence, there are a few technical specifications that our company must ensure you comply with.

- The advertisement must be no smaller than A4 and no larger than A3
- The date, times and location of performances must be clearly visible on the advertisement – the play will be performed at Glen Street Theatre, 8pm–10.30pm, 14–22 September 2017.
- The title of the play (*Macbeth*) and the name of the composer (William Shakespeare) must be included.
- A quote summing up the selected theme must feature on the advertisement.

Deliverables

PART A: You must submit a visual, static advertisement no smaller than A4 and no larger than A3.

Please note that posters should not contain 3D elements or elements that exceed the maximum A3 size limit.

Three Witches Theatre Co. (Continued)

PART B: All teams submitting for this design contract must pitch their design to a representative of the Three Witches Theatre Company. Each individual team member is required to present a two-minute justification of his/her artistic decisions (such as colours, symbols, layout, font) and how these communicate the team's selected theme and his/her personal interpretation of *Macbeth*.

NOTE: All entries including Parts A & B must be handed in to the English Staffroom on or before the closing date _____.

Further Information

For further information about this project, please speak with your classroom teacher or your peers in person or via your class Edmodo group.

What is the deadline for entries?

You have a four-week deadline for this project. The closing date for submission of designs and pitches is _____.

What are the judging criteria?

To help you compete to the highest level and give each team the best chance at winning this design contract, we have put together rigorous criteria to assist in assessing the quality of the work of the design team. Use the criteria below to help you plan, draft and revise your submission.

- sophisticated use of visual features (including symbols, colour, layout, salience, contrast, imagery) to create a cohesive design
- sophisticated understanding of how the elements of visual design can be used to inform, persuade and entertain
- sophisticated transformation of the ideas and style of *Macbeth* to meet the purpose, audience and context of the design
- composes a sophisticated design that demonstrates originality, imagination and ingenuity in content and construction
- design concept statement articulates an insightful understanding of Shakespeare's exploration of power within *Macbeth*
- design concept statement demonstrates a sophisticated understanding of the process of representation in texts
- ability to articulate and discuss the pleasures and difficulties, successes and challenges experienced in investigation, problem-solving, independent and collaborative work, and establish improved practices

NOTE: The top eight teams will pitch their design for an advertising campaign to a panel of judges on _____. On this day the winner of the design contract will be announced.

Three Witches Theatre Co.

Planning for Success

1. **SELECT YOUR DESIGN TEAM.** When choosing team members it is important to select individuals who have the skills to meet the demands of the task. Skills to include in your team include: creativity, organisation, collaboration, leadership, time-management and a sense of humour.

    NOTE: some teachers will select the design teams.

2. **FAMILIARISE YOURSELF WITH THE REQUIREMENTS OF THE TASK.** Re-read the design brief and be sure to ask your peers or teacher if you have any further questions. Make sure you pay close attention to the judging criteria.

3. **PLAN YOUR TIME.** You have four weeks until entries close. During this time you will need to complete the following:

    a. Familiarise yourself with the play *Macbeth* by William Shakespeare. You are required to understand the plot, characters, ideas relating to themes in the play and the use of imagery and symbols.

    b. Find evidence from the play to support your thoughts about your selected idea/theme explored within the play.

    c. Generate a list of images and symbols from the play that represent your selected theme/idea.

    d. Brainstorm how you can best represent your selected theme/idea in *Macbeth* in your design.

    e. Create a draft design – seek teacher and peer feedback.

    f. Create a polished advertisement to show during your 'pitch'.

    g. Write a draft design concept pitch – seek teacher and peer feedback.

    h. Create and rehearse a polished design concept pitch.

Use the calendar on Edmodo to help your Design Team plan your time leading up to the closing date. Alternatively, you may like to use your diary or a paper calendar.

4. **GET TO WORK**

REPRODUCIBLE – PART TWO: SAMPLE PROJECTS YEAR 10 – 3. SOMETHING WICKED

KWL TABLE

Use a KWL table like the one below to work out what you already know that will help you to succeed at **each** element of the task, what you want to learn and how you think you can learn what you need to in order to succeed.

What we Know	What we Want to Learn	How we Aim to Learn It

REPRODUCIBLE – PART TWO: SAMPLE PROJECTS YEAR 10 – 3. SOMETHING WICKED

BEFORE YOU BEGIN

CONTACT EXPERTS

There are a number of experts that you can get involved in this project. The point at which they are involved will be determined by the expert that you choose. Some possible experts include: the manager for a local theatre; advertising creative; Shakespeare expert; actor from local amateur theatre company; academic from nearby university.

PLAN THE HOOK LESSON

As always, there are a range of options for how to launch your project to engage your students' interests. You could focus on any element of the project, including the themes of *Macbeth*, aspects of Shakespeare's life or language, the theatre or advertising. The suggested hook lesson below focuses students on the themes from the play.

1. Sit students in Campfire arrangement.
2. Students are each given a Post-It note.
3. On the Post-It notes students write a type of 'power', e.g. supernatural, feminine.
4. Student post Post-Its to whiteboard.
5. Teacher hands Post-Its back to students randomly.
6. Students organise themselves into groups of 3–5 and select one of the powers on the Post-Its to act out for the class.
7. Students are sent outside to the school oval and given 15 minutes to plan and rehearse the power skit.
8. Students gather at outdoor amphitheatre.
9. Teacher gives each student a Post-It with a type of Elizabethan profession on it.
10. Students are to sit in the amphitheatre relative to the status of their Elizabethan profession (e.g. nobility sits on top tier, tradesmen etc. stand in front of 'stage').
11. Students watch as each group performs their power skit.
12. Audience guesses the type of power being represented.
13. Blind vote on the 'best' skit and award prize of chocolate to skit judged the best.

NEED TO KNOW – MACBETH

Does it have to be advertised in a certain way? What format? (computer, filmed etc.)

What power will our team be representing in our campaign and how will it be represented?

What are we advertising?

Is Part A as a team, or individual?

How do you advertise a theatre production?

How does female power affect Macbeth?

Who will be doing each task?

Who are the characters from *Macbeth*?

Will we need to include Macbeth in our advertisements?

How long will this project take?

How do we present the advertisement?

What are we trying to say about Macbeth?

Who are we aiming the advertisement at? How do we?

What does it mean by 'power'?

How long does the pitch need to be?

How big does the poster have to be?

To whom are we presenting our pitch?

What will our design look like?

Where do we get information?

What do we need to know about Shakespeare?

What is the play *Macbeth* about?

What makes a good advertising campaign?

DISCOVER

The first part of every project should be handing out the project outline and establishing what students feel they need to know to successfully complete the project. To help you understand the types of questions that students could be asking at the 'need to know' stage, look at the questions generated by my Year 10 students when they began this same project (on the following page). Don't give this copy to your class, rather use it as a teacher resource to help you guide your students to similar types of inquiry questions.

This project has an extended 'inquiry' phase because students must engage with a Shakespearean text. Of course, how you decide to get your students to engage with the texts is up to you and highly dependent on your students. Some teachers will want their students to engage with the written text through a whole-class close reading of the play. Some teachers will read extracts of the play but spend most of the time watching a film adaptation. Other teachers may have their students engage with the story of the play and watch YouTube videos that explain key aspects of the play. Ultimately, students are required to discover the play's plot, characters, themes and style through a process of inquiry, whether that is guided or independent. Performance of key scenes is a rewarding and challenging activity for students. Scenes to consider performing are: the opening scenes with the witches, Macbeth's soliloquy before he kills Duncan, the banquet after the murder of Banquo, the witches' apparitions and the death of Macbeth. I have had great success with students putting Post-It notes in their copies of the play to identify key scenes, symbols and imagery. This provides them with a useful resource when they come to creating their advertisement. A range of resources have been included to support your students' learning at this stage of the project.

FORMATIVE ASSESSMENT

Below are some strategies you might like to use to check students' understanding and skills at this stage of the project.

- Quiz students on their knowledge of the play (a quiz has been included).
- Check students' understanding of the play by looking at the quantity and quality of the Post-It notes in their copy of the play.

MACBETH QUIZ

1. Who said, 'If chance will have me king, why, chance may crown me'?
    a. Duncan
    b. Macbeth
    c. Banquo
    d. Malcolm

2. Who said, 'Are you a man?'
    a. Macbeth
    b. Duncan
    c. Lady Macbeth
    d. Malcolm

3. This play is often read as a cautionary tale against too much
    a. wife
    b. ambition
    c. greed
    d. temptation

4. The play opens with
    a. a battle
    b. witches
    c. dogs
    d. a banquet

5. What is the witches' mantra?
    a. fair is foul and foul is fair
    b. brew is the stew
    c. macbeth rules
    d. all is fair in love and war

6. What prophecy has been made about Macbeth?
    a. that he will be the chosen one
    b. that he will one day be King of Scotland
    c. that he will die young
    d. that he will prick his finger on a spinning wheel and fall into a deep sleep

7. What does Macbeth do to King Duncan?
    a. he frames him for the murder of the chamberlains
    b. he steals his watch
    c. he murders him
    d. he plays a practical joke on him

8. Whose ghost does Macbeth find seated at the royal table?
    a. King Duncan's
    b. King Hamlet's
    c. Banquo's
    d. Nearly Headless Nick's

9. Which symbols are used throughout the play *Macbeth*?
    a. storms, snakes, blood, clothing
    b. snakes, cats, night, roses
    c. shadows, blood, water, red
    d. clothing, snakes, butterflies, sand

10. How many iambs are there in iambic pentameter?
    a. 6
    b. 5
    c. 8
    d. 10

MACBETH QUIZ

11. Who speaks prose in *Macbeth*?
    a. Macbeth
    b. Porter
    c. Lady Macbeth
    d. Duncan

12. Which of these lines from the play below is a metaphor?
    a. 'If you can look into the seeds of time, And say which grain will grow and which will not, Speak then to me'
    b. 'My dearest love, Duncan comes here to-night.'
    c. 'Who can be wise, amazed, temperate and furious, Loyal and neutral, in a moment? No man'
    d. 'Thou canst not say I did it: never shake Thy gory locks at me.'

Identify three settings in the play *Macbeth*.
....
....
....

Identify four main characters from the play, *Macbeth*.
....
....
....

What are four different types of power explored in the play *Macbeth*? Describe a scene where each type of power in this play is evident.
....
....
....
....

What is the play *Macbeth* about? (Try to write about three sentences.)
....
....
....
....
....
....
....

How does female power affect Macbeth?
....
....
....
....

REPRODUCIBLE – PART TWO: SAMPLE PROJECTS YEAR 10 – 3. SOMETHING WICKED

MACBETH QUIZ
Defining Power

1. What does the word 'power' mean?
   ....
   ....
   ....

2. Find three definitions for the word 'power'.

3. Write the definitions below.

   a. ....
      ....
      ....

   b. ....
      ....
      ....

   c. ....
      ....
      ....

4. Now using this information, re-write your answer to question 1.
   ....
   ....
   ....
   ....
   ....
   ....
   ....

MACBETH QUIZ
Using Power

1. **Can power be used for good?**

    What are some examples of individuals or groups using power for good in our world? You can answer in dot points or in full sentences.

    - ....
    - ....
    - ....
    - ....
    - ....

2. **Can power be used for evil?**

    What are some examples of individuals or groups using power for evil in our world? You can answer in dot points or in full sentences.

    - ....
    - ....
    - ....
    - ....
    - ....

3. **What have people said about power in the past?**

    Find FIVE quotes from the Internet about power. You could try the following websites:

    www.quotegarden.com

    www.quotationspage.com

MACBETH QUIZ
Types of Power

There are four different types of power that can be identified:

- physical
- emotional/mental
- social
- supernatural

Tasks

1. Write a brief definition of each type of power. You can add an image or cartoon to support your definition if you like.

   - physical power
   - emotional power
   - social power
   - supernatural power

2. **Match the Powers**

   For each situation, write below it what type of power it represents.

   Situation 1:

   Chuck Norris picks up a car and throws it at an assailant.

   Situation 2:

   During the Apartheid era, black South Africans were forced to use separate public transport to white South Africans.

   Situation 3:

   In the movie *Ghost*, Patrick Swayze plays a character who moves a coin up a door without touching it.

   Situation 4:

   The song 'Eleanor Rigby' by The Beatles makes people cry.

MACBETH QUIZ

My Power

Are you a powerful person?

Tasks

1. **Write a few sentences explaining why you think you are or are not a powerful person.**

   Remember that your power may be: physical, emotional, mental, supernatural or social.

   ....

   ....

2. **Write a haiku that shows the type(s) of power you have. You can make it funny or serious – it's up to you.**

   What is a haiku?

   A haiku is an un-rhymed 17-syllable poem of Japanese origin. It usually has a seasonal reference. The structure is:

   - Line 1 – 5 syllables
   - Line 2 – 7 syllables
   - Line 3 – 5 syllables

   ....

   ....

   ....

   ....

3. **Share your haiku.**

   Share your haiku with someone else in the class. Write his/her haiku below:

   ....

   ....

   ....

   ....

   Continued

MACBETH QUIZ

My Power (Continued)

4. Power of persuasion

If you needed to get your own way in a situation, what kind of power would you use?

- Argument: 'I use my power to get my own way.'
- Write a 3-sentence paragraph that argues your point and provides supporting evidence.
- Use the following paragraph structure as a guide.

1. STATEMENT: Restate the question with your answer. E.g. 'I use my physical power to get my own way.'

2. SUPPORTIVE EVIDENCE: Briefly outline an example to support your point. E.g. 'This was evident when playing the grand final and I tackled the biggest guy on the field, stopping him from scoring a try.'

3. LINK BACK TO YOUR ARGUMENT: Explain how this example supports your argument. E.g. 'In conclusion I feel that my physical power is very useful in helping me get my own way.'

....

....

....

....

....

....

....

....

....

....

CREATE 🎵

The extended project outline given at the beginning of this project provides your students with a series of learning activities to support their learning during this project. Students will work in teams to design an advertising campaign for a theatre production of *Macbeth*. The advertisement can be created using a computer or drawn/painted by hand. It is a good idea for each team to select the same art style as this ensures cohesion between the advertisements. Students will be pitching their designs as a team, so they must work hard to show that their advertisements are part of a cohesive campaign. Encourage students to consider the context of their advertisement and how that will affect its design, e.g. advertisements on a bus shelter, in a magazine, on social media or a flyer for letterboxes. I recommend that each advertisement within a campaign have the same colour scheme, font, theatre company logo and information about the performance. Some handouts about Shakespeare's use of imagery and symbols in *Macbeth* are included to support your students with their designs. Each team should plan their advertisements and create a rough draft before seeking teacher feedback to make sure they're on the right track.

You will likely need to run an explicit lesson on how to write a rationale. It is up to you whether you refer to this as a design concept statement (the term used in the advertising industry) or if you stick with the term rationale, which is more commonly used in English classes. A handout giving a suggested structure for a rationale, as well as a student sample, has been included to help with this step.

Students should write a draft rationale and seek teacher feedback to help identify any gaps or areas for improvement.

IMAGERY

Shakespeare's plays are dense with imagery. He has many of his main characters speak with beautifully poetic voices. Some poetic devices that you may have noticed as you read through *Macbeth* include metaphor, simile, personification, hyperbole, onomatopoeia and alliteration.

These techniques are used to create mood and imagery. The type of imagery used by each character also reflects their personality and affects the way that we view them.

See if you can find examples of the following type of imagery as you flick back through the play.

Disease Imagery

Example:

....

....

....

Natural Imagery

Example:

....

....

....

Death Imagery

Example:

....

....

....

Night and Day Imagery

Example:

....

....

....

Blood Imagery

Example:

....

....

....

Animal Imagery

Example:

....

....

....

Supernatural Imagery

Example:

....

....

....

REPRODUCIBLE – PART TWO: SAMPLE PROJECTS YEAR 10 – 3. SOMETHING WICKED

SYMBOLS

Shakespeare loves to use symbols in his plays. It becomes like a game trying to spot each symbol and trying to figure out what it means. Shakespeare is sometimes hard for people to understand because he can be really tricky with his symbols – they are often ambiguous (this just means really hard to work out, and sometimes unclear).

Here are some frequently used symbols in *Macbeth*. For each one, identify a time when it is used in *Macbeth*, then try to work out what it is symbolic of and what Shakespeare is trying to tell us by using it in certain scenes.

Bloody Daggers

....
....
....

Hands

....
....
....

Crowns/Kings

....
....
....

Babies/Children

....
....
....

Clothing

....
....
....

REPRODUCIBLE – PART TWO: SAMPLE PROJECTS YEAR 10 – 3. SOMETHING WICKED

WRITING YOUR RATIONALE

The final part of the Visual Representation task is to reflect on your design.

THE TASK

Compose a 300-word rationale clearly explaining the intentions of your visual representation. You must outline how your image/s represent the theme you have chosen. Justify the choices you have made in terms of your use of colour, framing, symbolism, high/low modality, salience, gaze and vectors.

STATEMENT: Open with a really strong statement – this is your chance to **tell me what your poster is about** – that will mention the power you have chosen to represent. Try to include abstract nouns such as 'corruption', 'deception' and 'manipulation'. Here is an example based on the visual representation below: 'William Shakespeare's tragedy *King Lear* is a confronting exploration of the futility of the human experience and the impotence of man in the face of a chaotic, unstable and uncertain universe.'

TECHNIQUE: Tell me about THREE visual techniques that you have used to represent your chosen power. For example, in the poster below I would talk about symbolism, background and vectors. For each technique explain WHY it has been chosen and HOW it relates to the events of the play. Try to include a quote from the play to support each technique. Remember EACH one of these techniques needs to be discussed SEPARATELY.

GET TO WORK

VISUAL REPRESENTATION RATIONALE

William Shakespeare's play *Macbeth* revolves around the ambitions of the once brave and valiant Macbeth and how his actions lead to his tragic downfall and the destruction of his personality. My advertisement represents ideas relating to the illegitimate power of Macbeth and the legitimate power of Malcolm.

Malcolm is portrayed as a lone flower that has broken through Macbeth's failed attempt to rule over Scotland through illegitimate power. However Macbeth (portrayed as a snake) is trying to sneak up from hell and recapture this power. Malcolm is surviving with help from the angels who are drawing him toward the heavens, and consequently giving him the legitimate power to rule, reflective of the Elizabethan belief that sovereignty was thought to have been determined by God.

In my advertisement, the inclusion of the fiery flames symbolises the evilness of hell but they also act as vectors to draw the attention of the viewer upward. The hands (also in the symbolic colours of evil) symbolise the evilness trying to draw Malcolm down toward them but the angels helping Malcolm are illustrated by the colours white and silver to symbolise their purity. Both of these groups of images are vectors leading to Malcolm, illustrating the division between Malcolm and Macbeth, and consequently the division of legitimate and illegitimate power. Also, the turquoise (sovereignty and purity) flower is another salient image on the page that draws the viewer's attention to the face of Malcolm, the centre of the flower situated at the top of the stem. This stem works as another vector, drawing the viewer's attention away from the flower to the snake wrapped around the stem and attempting to sneak up on Malcolm.

Consequently my advertisement portrays my belief that legitimate power will succeed over illegitimate power in ruling over a country. I believe this advertisement would appeal to an audience of young adults (17–24 years of age) because individuals in this age group often experience concerns about status and how to increase their status. The image I have chosen is simple and strong, which would make the advertisement visually appealing to a younger demographic.

FORMATIVE ASSESSMENT

This project is driven by quality teamwork. Give students the opportunity to comment on their collaborative skills (and focus them on their role in the group) by giving them a mini reflection task like the one below. My students completed this activity at the end of a lesson.

Three things I did this lesson to help develop my team's advertising campaign were

1. ....
   ....

2. ....
   ....

3. ....
   ....

Signed: (all team members and teacher)

SHARE

The final presentation for this project is a very formal event. Students must ensure that they are aware of the importance of a pitch, and that they are being given a wonderful opportunity to learn how to sell themselves and their ideas – this will be an experience they must repeat many times when they leave school, or even before. It is a good idea to set up the space for the pitch like an interview. Sit you and the guest expert on one side of a large table (acting as representatives of the Three Witches Theatre Company) with the team of students on the other side. Each team member should speak about one of the advertisements – usually this is the one they have designed themselves – and share their reasons why they think it is effective and contributes to the team's overall design for the advertising campaign. You and the invited expert should take notes on each team's pitch (a resource has been provided for this) because at the end only one team will 'win' the design contract. It is a nice touch to have the invited expert give a symbolic 'contract' to the winning team and explain the reasons for the team's success.

YEAR 10
4. WILD AT HEART

PROJECT AT A GLANCE

 **DRIVING QUESTION:** Are humans wild at heart?

 DISCOVER: Students will research Freud's structural model of the mind (id, ego, superego), and the language forms and features of both texts, as well as discovering how to write a personal essay.

CREATE: Students will individually compose a personal essay answering the driving question.

 SHARE: The class will publish an anthology of their personal essays using Blurb or a similar online book publisher. The published book will go on display at the school or local library.

 ASSESSMENT: Students will be assessed on their personal essay – the plan, draft and final product.

 21ST-CENTURY SKILLS: critical thinking, ethical understanding

LITERACY: grammar – sentence structure, passive/active voice; spelling – nominalisations; punctuation – ellipses, semicolons

MODES: reading, writing, viewing

TYPES OF TEXT: informative (personal essay) and imaginative (picture book and film)

LANGUAGE FEATURES OF TEXTS: personal essay structure, voice, rhetorical devices, themes, visual techniques (layout, texture, modality, colour, gaze, vectors, salience, symbols, shots, angles)

READING/COMPREHENSION: making connections and questioning

TEXTS: *Where the Wild Things Are* by Maurice Sendak; *Where the Wild Things Are* by Spike Jonze.

ARE HUMANS WILD AT HEART?

INQUIRE

1. Complete the KWL table about this project.

2. Investigate Sigmund Freud's structural model of the psyche.

3. Conduct a critical comparison of the picture book *Where the Wild Things Are* by Maurice Sendak, and its film adaptation directed by Spike Jonze.

PRODUCE

1. Research, draft and edit a personal essay answering the driving question. Draw evidence to support your argument from Sendak's picture book, Jonze's film and at least one other text studied so far this year. You will be allocated a mentor to help you with this process.

PRESENT

1. Publish your personal essay in a class collection to be made available in the school's library.

2. Present your completed essay to an audience of invited guests.

REPRODUCIBLE – PART TWO: SAMPLE PROJECTS YEAR 10 – 4. WILD AT HEART

BEFORE YOU BEGIN

CONTACT EXPERTS

For this project you may wish to involve content experts or form experts. The content of this project is, mostly, related to psychology and how context impacts human behaviour and decisions. In relation to this aspect of the project you may wish to involve ex-students currently studying psychology at university or an academic or expert in the work of Freud or Jung. Another element is the form of the texts being studied – a picture book and a film. You may wish to involve an academic who specialises in picture books or films, or who is well acquainted with the work of Spike Jonze or Maurice Sendak. The final element of the project is the form of the product being created – a personal essay. You may choose to involve a published essayist or a blogger. Personal essays have a lot in common with blogging in terms of structure and style.

PLAN THE HOOK LESSON

For this project, a hook lesson involving play is essential as it relates to the core ideas of both the picture book and the film. Organise a range of childhood games for students to play, such as:

- dress-ups
- playing tip
- skipping
- hopscotch
- building cubbies/forts
- finger painting
- making mud pies
- playing with Play-doh
- doing craft with crepe paper.

DISCOVER

This stage of the project will include teacher-directed and student-directed learning. Looking at the project outline, it is clear to see that there are three main elements to the inquiry for this project. How much support and direction you give students in their inquiry is dependent on the skill level of your students. Here is a quick overview of what students will need to 'discover' at this stage of the project.

- Freud's structural model of the psyche. This is essentially focusing on his division of the mind into three parts – the id, the ego and the superego – and his ideas relating to the conscious and unconscious mind. Focus specifically on his ideas about repression because these relate directly to the two texts being studied and the notion of being 'wild at heart'. Students can access this information on the Internet, although you will need to speak with them about what they might find – we know some of Freud's theories get a bit racy. Another way to engage students with this information is through YouTube videos. There are some great ones out there, you just have to find them.

- The two texts and the biography of each artist. Maurice Sendak's biography is particularly interesting and there are a number of really insightful critical reviews of his picture book available on the Internet. Students will likely need to spend time refreshing their knowledge of visual literacy devices and the five elements of narrative. Similarly, the biography of Spike Jonze and his post-modern context are great discussion points as they impact the composition of his film adaptation of the picture book. Students will likely need to spend time refreshing their knowledge of film techniques. After responding to each text, request that students write a 300-word review of each text, making reference to the context of each composer.
- The language and structure of a personal essay. There is a useful handout for this in the resources for the *Romeo and Juliet* project earlier in this book.
- A film techniques quiz has been included – use it as a pre- or post-test.

FILM TECHNIQUES QUIZ

1. What shot type is used in the example?
    a. long-shot
    b. medium-shot
    c. close-up
    d. extreme long-shot

2. What shot type is used in the example?
    a. medium long-shot
    b. medium shot
    c. close-up
    d. big close-up

3. What shot type is used in the example?
    a. extreme close-up
    b. big close-up
    c. close-up
    d. extreme long-shot

4. What shot type is used in the example?
    a. long shot
    b. medium shot
    c. close-up
    d. extreme long-shot

REPRODUCIBLE — PART TWO: SAMPLE PROJECTS YEAR 10 — 4. WILD AT HEART

FILM TECHNIQUES QUIZ

5. What shot type is used in the example?
    a. extreme long-shot
    b. long-shot
    c. medium long-shot
    d. medium shot

6. What shot type is used in the example?
    a. extreme long-shot
    b. big close-up
    c. close-up
    d. medium close-up

7. What shot type is used in the example?
    a. long shot
    b. extreme close-up
    c. close-up
    d. medium long-shot

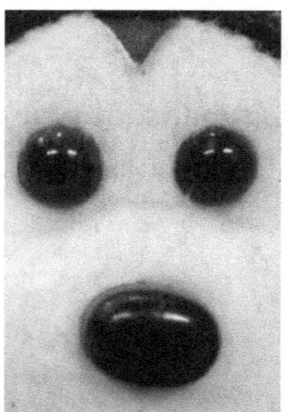

8. Which camera angle is being used in the example?
    a. high-angle shot
    b. low-angle shot
    c. canted
    d. over-head shot

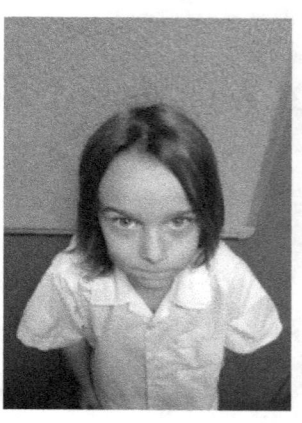

REPRODUCIBLE – PART TWO: SAMPLE PROJECTS YEAR 10 – 4. WILD AT HEART

FILM TECHNIQUES QUIZ

9. Which camera angle is being used in the example?
    a. high-angle shot
    b. low-angle shot
    c. eye-level shot
    d. bird's eye shot

10. Which camera angle is being used in the example?
    a. high-angle shot
    b. low-angle shot
    c. eye-level shot
    d. worm's eye

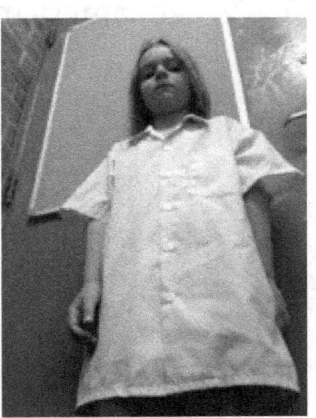

11. Which camera angle is being used in the example?
    a. worm's eye
    b. low-angle shot
    c. eye-level shot
    d. over-head shot

12. Which camera angle is being used in the example?
    a. canted
    b. low-angle shot
    c. eye-level shot
    d. bird's eye shot

REPRODUCIBLE – PART TWO: SAMPLE PROJECTS YEAR 10 – 4. WILD AT HEART

FILM TECHNIQUES QUIZ

13. Which camera angle is being used in the example?
    a. high-angle shot
    b. low-angle shot
    c. eye-level shot
    d. canted

14. What camera movement technique would be used in a chase scene?
    a. tracking shot
    b. tilt
    c. panning
    d. dolly shot

15. What type of camera movement would be used to reveal the setting of a scene?
    e. tracking shot
    f. tilt
    g. panning
    h. dolly shot

BACK-LIGHTING   PANNING
TILT   ZOOMING
LOW KEY   HIGH KEY
                 TRACKING

16. Fill in the spaces in the sentences below using words from the box above.

    In _____ the camera does not move; the lens is focused down from a long-shot to a close-up while the picture is still being shown.

    _____ is a vertical movement of the camera – up or down – while the camera mounting stays fixed.

    _____ involves the camera itself being moved smoothly towards or away from the subject.

    In a _____ shot the camera swivels (in the same base position) to follow a moving subject.

    _____ lighting is bright and relatively low in contrast.

    _____ lighting creates pronounced shadows and dramatic contrasts.

    _____ produces a 'halo' effect around the edges of the subject.

REPRODUCIBLE – PART TWO: SAMPLE PROJECTS YEAR 10 – 4. WILD AT HEART

CREATE 🎵

There are a number of collaborative learning and critical thinking strategies you can use to get students to develop their ideas about the two texts and the driving question. You may wish to use some of these: think/pair/share, starbursting, hexagonal thinking, lotus diagrams, hot potato, jigsaws or Venn diagrams.

To support students with understanding what should or could be included in their personal essay, you may like to give them the 'What are some things I should talk about in my personal essay?' information which can be seen below.

Students will work in critical friend teams to plan, draft and edit their individual personal essays. Encourage students to read each other's plans and drafts, and to give constructive feedback using the 'praise, inform, praise' or 'star, star, wish' feedback method. This will allow students to give both positive and constructive feedback. To develop peer-assessment skills, you might like to model how to do it using the sample student personal essay included. The included personal essay checklist (p. 33) can be useful for this activity as well.

If you have a very capable class, extend their learning and writing by requesting that they write about the two given texts as well as an additional text they have already studied in English that year. You will see that the sample personal essay included has been written in this way.

What are some things I should talk about in my personal essay?

1. *Make sure your essay answers the driving question: Are humans wild at heart?*

This is a personal essay – this means you get to write about your own thoughts, opinions and experiences on the issue. The issue that you need to focus on is what constitutes being 'wild' and whether this is a normal part of human nature. Your essay may focus on the fact that we are not 'wild' as this part of us is normal, or you may argue that it is an unnatural, unhealthy aspect of our nature that needs to be dealt with somehow. You may argue that there is no right or wrong way to be.

Brainstorm your personal ideas about what 'wild' might mean for you. For example, is it our

- unconscious, instinctual drive to fulfil our own needs or desires (what Freud called our 'id')?
- repressed, unconscious memories?
- socially unacceptable thoughts and desires (what Freud called 'taboo')?
- fears (of change, loss, uncertainty)?
- primitive longing for freedom?
- true self, free from the bondage of anxiety and self-consciousness?

2. *Brainstorm ways in which our 'wild' side may present itself (what Freud calls 'manifestation'). For example, in our*

- dreams
- art
- misbehaviour
- arguments

- rejection of social expectations
- rebellion

3. When you have decided on what you would like to focus on in your personal essay – your argument answering the driving question – you should think about identifying a few examples from texts to support your ideas. You need to find supporting examples from the picture book, Where the Wild Things Are, the film Where the Wild Things Are and one other text you have studied this year in English. Try to add quotes, descriptions of images or scenes and a discussion of HOW ideas have been represented in these texts. Note: HOW = techniques and effects.

4. Your personal essay should feature the introduction, body, conclusion structure BUT your paragraphs can be quite loosely structured. There is no need to use the STEEL paragraph structure. Make sure each idea expressed in your paragraphs is supported with an example – this could be from one of the texts you have studied or from your own experience in life or from an idea of Freud's. You should try to write at least THREE body paragraphs.

5. Focus on making your personal essay engaging – use the language features suggested on the 'Overview of the Personal Essay' handout.

Sample Personal Essay

By Loren Holley

When pondering the nature of human beings, it is rather easy to start putting people in boxes. It is easy to forget that we are all different in some way and no two of us are the same. At least, that's what I've been told my entire life. However, surely there is something which is common to each of us? Something which is universal? Well, in fact, there is. In my experience, once you get past our surface characteristics, humans have something very major in common. Somewhere, within each of us, is an aspect that is separate from the influences of our context. This part of our minds expresses itself through different mediums in our lives: our dreams, our actions and our art. Often, we don't even realise it's there. It is a feature that is common to each of us and as a result links us together as a species. Each of us, every single human being, is wild at heart.

When I use the term wild, I'm meaning the part of each of us that tells us how to feel, how to act and how to behave according to what best suits us. In my opinion, our 'wild side' comprises the basic survival impulses that we all possess. Once you strip away all the surface features that make each of us different, you are left with these common subconscious drives. Whether we act upon them or not is our choice. Many people opt to repress this 'wild side', choosing instead to govern their behaviour in a 'socially appropriate' way. Others constantly act upon their impulses and face the consequences of what is considered to be 'socially inappropriate'. But what would I know? Well, this concept of each of us having a 'wild' aspect to our mind is expressed time and time again within literature and art.

For me, the perfect example of a person who represses their 'wild side' is that of the Unknown Citizen, the central character from W. H. Auden's poem of the same name. The poem is centred on the life of an unidentified man and written from the perspective of an inscription on the man's funeral monument. We pick up very quickly that this inscription has been written, not by a loved one, but from the point of view of a governmental organisation simply referred to as 'The State'. I believe that this perspective is a stroke of genius on Auden's part. It creates an impersonal relationship with the Unknown Citizen which is very necessary for developing a sense of his submissive nature. For you see, from the very first stanza to the very last, we pick up that this man was effectively the ideal citizen: a perfect consumer, a perfect worker and the perfect cog in The State's machine. Line after line details his many 'achievements', including his ability to 'hold the proper opinions for the time of year' and to 'react to advertisements in a normal way'. Auden's clever use of irony when describing the Unknown citizen highlights how he stifles his wild side in order to achieve social conformity.

Despite Auden's tone, it is apparent to me that the State is thrilled with this man's contribution towards the 'Greater Community'. By repeating terms such as 'sensible' and 'satisfactory', Auden has managed to paint a picture in my mind of the Unknown Citizen's ability to be suitably unremarkable in the eyes of The State. For me, this clearly creates a sense of the man himself, albeit from an outside perspective. I think this links strongly with the idea of repressing one's natural impulses in order to achieve social acceptance. On top of this, Auden has developed an impression of the oppressed society in which the Unknown Citizen lived, a society that Auden doubtlessly had experience with considering that this poem was written during WWII. It is highly likely that The Unknown Citizen is in fact a reflection of people that Auden had experience with in his everyday life.

All of this demonstrates that Auden's Unknown Citizen is a reflection of the repressed attitude that many people possess. He is effectively someone who does everything for everyone else, living to serve The State and conform to the Greater Community, rather than indulging in his own desires. He is also an embodiment of a part of each of us. He is the part that tells us to keep our heads down and not make a fuss. In other words, he is a representation of our survival instincts. Because of this, in the Unknown Citizen we can see a hidden true nature, or wild side.

For a bolder expression of the wild heart within each of us, I need look no further than Max, the central character of the picture book and film *Where the Wild Things Are*. Written and illustrated in the 1960s by Maurice Sendak, the book follows the story of an energetic and, in some senses, arrogant young boy who finds himself in solitary confinement after behaving like a 'wild thing'. A real sense of Max's character is built through the book's vivid illustrations. He is constantly represented clad in his white wolf suit with a haughty look on his face. In my opinion, the most classic expression of his attitude is a delightful image of him leaping down the stairs, brandishing a fork and in obvious pursuit of the family dog. Naturally, this behaviour is deemed socially inappropriate and Max faces the consequences. His mother calls him a 'WILD THING' and he is sent to his room without any dinner. However, Max decides to take his isolation, not as a punishment, but as an opportunity to have some fun. As a result, he is depicted retreating into an imaginary world in which he is ruler – the place where the wild things are. The 'wild things' in question are hideous and appear to have been cobbled together from bits of other animals to form nightmarish creatures that could only exist within the realm of imagination. Max is not intimidated, tames them into submission by commanding them to 'BE STILL' and is crowned the king of all wild things.

Sendak's use of visual symbolism, such as the growth of the forest within his room and the recurring image of his wolf suit, really builds a sense of this little boy's perspective in my mind. To Max, the world should be a certain way. He refuses to accept his mother's desire for him to be different and the wild things are a reflection of this. This world, in which Max is king, is a place where being wild is revered and accepted rather than shunned. Sendak communicates this concept through the contrast between the place where the wild things are and Max's bedroom. The vibrantly coloured overgrowth of the forest in comparison with the orderly state of his room demonstrates the difference between Max's ideal world and his reality. This is an example of how our wild side comprises our basic survival impulses and I can relate quite strongly to Max's desire to control his surroundings. After all, it is a natural part of human instinct.

The film interpretation, though remarkably true to the book, delves deeper into Max's need for control by introducing a fundamental resistance to change within the character. On top of this, I found this interpretation to have a much stronger dream-like quality than the picture book. The director, Spike Jonze, has chosen to represent Max as being fatherless, with a stressed-out Mum and a distant sister. To me, all of this hints at some aspect of Max's life having massively changed within recent times. However right from the opening scene, where Max is ferociously playing with the family dog, we pick up that he has not changed with it. Spike Jonze continues with his interpretation of the story by introducing the Mum as having a new boyfriend. It is apparent that Max feels highly threatened by him and, while donning his white wolf suit, he defies his mother in an attempt to draw her attention. A fight ensues and Max flees from the house into the night street. At this point, I particularly appreciated Jonze's use of jerky camera movements and animalistic music to set the mood. It really created an impression of Max's reaction being linked with something deeper than conscious, logical thought which links back to the concept of our natural subconscious wild side.

I feel that the next major reflection of this is with the introduction of the character Carol, a wild thing who is doubtlessly a personification of the 'wild' aspect of Max's personality. By this point, Max is huddled in the forest of the place where the wild things are. Peering out timidly, he sees Carol violently demolishing his surroundings. Max seems to resonate with Carol on some level about this destruction and he rushes out to join in. Personally, I found this act to be symbolic of the relationship that would form between Max and Carol. Throughout the film, Jonze has used many subtle techniques to highlight Max's reluctance towards change. For example, the desert that repeatedly features is symbolic of the passage of time, as it is represented through the quote 'this land used to be rock, now it is sand, then it will be dust and not even I know what comes after dust'. Also, the wild thing KW is constantly at odds with Carol over the introduction of her friends, Bob and Terry. This is doubtlessly representative of Max's reaction to the change in his sister and their estranged relationship.

As the film progresses, Max seems to reach a place of understanding that allows him to deliberate his surroundings in a way that he was previously unable to. Carol, however, remains impulsive and aggressive and their relationship begins to fall apart. This, I felt, was a very clever representation of the consequences of constantly giving in to one's wild side. Thanks to his impulsivity, Carol cannot adapt to his surroundings. Eventually, Max decides to leave the place where the wild things are and return to his home. I feel that this was marvellously represented, with Carol remaining on the beach as Max sails away, and symbolic of him leaving behind this part of himself. All in all, Jonze has created a magnificent representation of Max's reactions to the world around him. These reactions stem from Max's subconscious mind as is represented through the dream-like quality of the film. As a result, Max is the perfect example of someone who acts upon the wild aspect that is common to each of us.

Although the characters of The Unknown Citizen and Max are radically exaggerated, I think that each of us can relate to them in some way. They both provide examples of the reactions that stem from our natural instincts and reveal the fact that we are indeed wild at heart. They are also examples of the consequences of both repressing our wild side and of letting it rule our heads. From them we can learn a valuable lesson. The key is to find the balance between the Unknown Citizen and Max. When we find this balance, the wild side within each of us can be one of our most precious resources. With too much wild or too little, we are limited in our perspectives. But with balance, we are able to tap into our raw emotions, the impulses that allow us to thrive and flourish as a species.

Personal Essay: Feedback

Name:

	Criteria	Teacher/Peer Feedback			I used feedback to improve		
		Still learning	Achieved	Above & Beyond	Didn't	Tried	Did
1	Does the essayist establish a personal and distinctive voice throughout the essay?						
2	Are a variety of sentence types used to create pace, mood and focus? Sentence types include simple, compound, complex.						
3	Is interesting, varied and appropriate vocabulary used to help the reader better understand the ideas of the personal essay?						
4	Does the essayist answer the driving question by presenting a personal and thoughtful argument?						
5	Does the introduction hint at the ideas in the body and/or directly engage with the driving question?						
6	Are the language features of an essay used to effectively engage readers? Language features may include emotive language, humour, symbolism, figurative language, humour, juxtaposition, first-person narrative, personal, subjective voice and/or modality.						
7	Does the personal essay have correct grammar, punctuation, spelling and paragraphing?						
8	Do body paragraphs present thoughtful and personal ideas that relate to the driving question?						
9	Do body paragraphs provide evidence to support the ideas being discussed in the paragraph?						
10	Does the conclusion of the essay provoke readers' thoughts/emotions/imagination and make them want to continue reading or ask questions of the essayist?						

Medals: (main strengths)

Missions: (improvements needed for this essay)

SHARE

This is quite an academic and intellectually challenging project. The concepts are complex and the way that the texts are engaged with is difficult. For many students, just getting their personal essay written will be cause for celebration. To show how you value the challenge your students have undergone and the work that they have produced, organise for the essays to be collected into a 'Wild Things' anthology and published as a hard cover book. We have used the online publisher Blurb in the past, with fantastic results. The book can be kept in the school library to be borrowed by students. Parents and friends can purchase copies from Blurb as well, as they make a great gift.

To further celebrate your students' achievements, invite your guest expert back to hear readings from selected personal essays. Organise one or two students to speak about the project – reflecting on what they enjoyed and what they found challenging. Friends and family could be invited as well, and they will certainly be impressed by what your students have learned during this project.

FORMATIVE ASSESSMENT

The final personal essays can be assessed using a modified version of the 'personal essay checklist' included on page 33.

YEAR 10

5. ENGLISH COMPOSITION PROJECT (ECP)

PROJECT AT A GLANCE

 **DRIVING QUESTION:** Students generate their own driving questions.

 DISCOVER: Students research a topic of interest and the most effective form to communicate this interest. Research will also be into text form, structure and language features as well as a potential audience for their composition, including publications/publishers.

 CREATE: Students will produce a 3000-word composition: this can be a collection of shorter pieces (poets, bloggers*, playwright, journalists, comic, authors, essayists) OR a 5-minute short film (film-makers) OR a 5-minute documentary (documentary-makers) plus 700-word process reflection.

* at least one blog post needs to be re-blogged or commented upon by a well-established blogger who writes about a similar topic

 SHARE: Students are to seek publication for their work (include rejection/acceptance letters in your portfolio) AND share part of their composition at the 'Publish or Perish Picnic' with peers.

 ASSESSMENT: Students will be assessed on their report, draft, final composition, process reflection and learning journal.

 21ST-CENTURY SKILLS: Collaboration, Creativity, Critical Thinking

LITERACY: grammar/spelling/punctuation/reading: (negotiated with teacher)

MODES: possible – reading, writing, viewing, listening, representing, speaking

TYPES OF TEXT: informative (research report), imaginative OR persuasive (ECP)

LANGUAGE FEATURES OF TEXTS: dependent on student topic of interest and selected text form

Publish or Perish

All throughout the year your study of English has been controlled by your English teacher: what texts you read or viewed and what texts you wrote or created. Well, that's all about to change. This project puts you in the hot seat as you finally get to compose in a form you love about ideas that interest YOU. That's right … over the next seven weeks you will be a poet, playwright, filmmaker, journalist, documentary-maker, blogger, poet, speech-writer, author, critic or essayist.

Research

- establish a driving question for your project
- research the central concept of your composition
- research the features, structures, conventions of your chosen form
- research your chosen audience: their needs, interests, expectations PLUS possible publication avenues
- find an expert mentor to support you through the composition process

Note: the research process will be recorded in your Process Journal — this may be digital or paper.

Compose

- 3000-word composition: this can be a collection of shorter pieces (poets, bloggers, playwright, journalists, speech-writers, authors, essayists) OR a 5-minute short-film (film-makers) OR a 5-minute documentary (documentary-makers)
- 700-word process reflection

Share

- seek publication for your work (include rejection/acceptance letters in your portfolio)
- present your composition at the 'Publish or Perish?' showcase

Some of the things you will learn

- research skills
- the joys and challenges of the composition process
- features and structures of your selected form
- how to manage your time and work to a deadline
- presentation skills
- creative thinking
- critical thinking
- persistence

REPRODUCIBLE — PART TWO: SAMPLE PROJECTS YEAR 10 — 5. ENGLISH COMPOSITION PROJECT

BEFORE YOU BEGIN

CONTACT EXPERTS

This project is all about mentors. As a teacher, you have a network full of potential mentors, much greater than that of your students. Use your networking powers for good. Edmodo, Twitter, Facebook, professional organisations – use all of them. Pre-service teachers from your local university would be great for this role. Each student requires a mentor. I have used my teacher blog to find mentors from all over the world for my students. For this project each student will decide on the concept and form for their composition. It is essential that mentors feel they have a choice in which student they mentor and should choose based on their area of expertise and/or interests. The role of the mentor is supportive more than anything else – they will be there throughout the project to provide your students with advice, to read over plans and drafts and to provide times for constructive criticism and praise.

The next experts to be involved are potential publishers. This part is entirely the responsibility of the students – identifying potential publishers is part of the research process. Both types of experts are vital to the success of this project as students will come to value themselves more as composers when others value them.

PLAN THE HOOK LESSON

Getting students engaged in this project shouldn't be too difficult because it is a project that involves a lot of choice and freedom. One way that I have engaged student interest is to create a video mash-up of photos of people who were successful at a young age. The purpose of this is to inspire students to see themselves as having the potential to be successful now, without having to wait until they are 'older'. Another possibility is having a range of creative 'stations' set up around the classroom, where students get to engage with/create a range of forms – film, blogs, picture books, comics, poetry, short stories etc.

DISCOVER

The following three-page handout provides students with some useful tips for how to begin their research and establish their concept. This is a heavily student-directed project, with you, the teacher, adopting the role of learning guide. Some students will require much greater support than others as they choose their form and concept together. At this early planning stage of the project, group those who are having trouble together. Spend one or two lessons with them brainstorming their interests and strengths. The 'research' aspect of this project involves students learning about:

- their chosen form (structure, language features, genre conventions)
- chosen concept
- publication possibilities.

FORMATIVE ASSESSMENT

Throughout this project, students will be reflecting on their learning in a learning journal. It is a good idea to check this each week and address any concerns that you have about their learning through a comment in their journal, or through a conversation in class. It's important that students see that you are reading this, as this will make them value it and use it more regularly. You may also want to have students write a brief plan or report about their chosen form and concept — you will need to give approval for their choices.

THE ITTY BITTY GRITTY DETAILS OF THE ECP

RESEARCH TIPS

- always record the source of your information correctly. Record this information: name of text/article/website, name of author, year of publication, page number, name of publisher and date accessed (for websites only)
- correctly reference all of your sources at the end of your process reflection: use *www.bibme.org*
- always check the reliability of your source (especially websites) by checking name of author, date of publication and name of publisher — are these reputable sources?
- for a more detailed guide to research, ask your teacher for a copy of the 'Research Guide'

TIPS FOR CRAFTING A 'DRIVING QUESTION'

- It's a good idea to have an 'action'-oriented driving question as this keeps you focused and motivated
- A good start to your driving question is 'How can I …'
- Here is an example: 'How can I write a novella that will impress a publisher?'

TIPS FOR DECIDING ON A 'CONCEPT'

- the concept for your composition is its main idea or message
- think of the main idea explored in the texts you have studied so far this year, for example the power of the imagination is explored in *Macbeth*
- think about what you find fascinating in life or in your favourite novel, video game, film or television show
- some examples might be: depression in young people, how authors control the responses of their readers, materialism, the bond between siblings or trauma after a break-up

TIPS FOR FINDING YOUR 'MENTOR'

- Your mentor can be someone who you know well, a friend of a friend/family member or someone you have never met.
- If you plan to connect with someone you have never met (such as a games designer or a film producer) remember that contact should not be face to face unless you have the approval of your parents/guardians.
- Take a risk and email or use social media to contact an expert in your chosen form and ask them to give you feedback or tips for your composition — make sure you have the approval of your parents/guardians first.
- Try asking another teacher at school — there are lots of experts at school.

POETS

- a single poem of 3000 words that could take the form of an epic/ballad.
- a suite of no more than 10 poems that must be connected via a central theme or motif

BLOGGERS

- a series of blog posts – no less than five and more than ten
- include hyperlinks and images with copyright attribution where appropriate

CRITICS/ESSAYISTS

This form gives you scope to discuss a whole world of ideas that can relate back to English. Remember that your writing needs to relate to concepts/texts studied in English this year. Don't see this as limiting but rather an opportunity to think creatively about English. Below is a list of possible research focus/questions for a critical response/essay. Each one is linked to a text studied this year.

MACBETH

Representations of women in platform games.

Symbols of light and dark in productions of Shakespeare's *Macbeth*.

MEDIA

Video game criticism in Australia.

Video games: the 21st century's most popular art form?

FILM

Inspirational teachers in Australian literature.

A comparison of the role of music in Australian and American film.

NOVEL/RESILIENCE

Representations of depression in young adult fiction.

Identity in massively multi-player online role-playing games.

Female protagonists in science fiction novels.

POETRY

What is the place of contemporary poets in 21st century Australia?

The changing relationship between poet and landscape in Australian poetry.

Aussie hip-hop: the new Australian poetry?

Tracing the roots of contemporary music in traditional musical forms

PROCESS REFLECTION

This is a 700-word overview of your project, explaining:

- the concept you aimed to explore in your composition
- your target audience, important sources that influenced your composition
- the relationship between your composition and texts/concepts studied in English this year
- obstacles and challenges you faced during the process and how you overcame these

THE 'PROCESS JOURNAL'

- each English lesson, set goals and reflect on your achievements using the 'goals/medals/missions' scaffold
- each entry needs to be dated
- write at least four entries per week
- entries should be personal and honest: write in the first-person
- include anything relevant to your project: sketches of your ideas, notes relating to research you have conducted, photographs, people's names, excerpt from texts, your fear and your joy

CREATE

The only explicit teaching lessons that you will need to do during this project include teaching referencing, how to keep a journal and how to contact and communicate with a mentor and potential publisher.

You may find that you need to run lessons with small groups of students who are all doing the same type of text (film, comics etc.). This may take the form of a writers' workshop or a lecture, depending on the identified student needs. It's likely you will help these small groups with grammar and punctuation relevant to their chosen form, as well as the language and structure of that form.

FORMATIVE ASSESSMENT

Below are some strategies you might like to use to check students' understanding and skills at this stage of the project.

- Different checklists for each type of text. The best way to do this is to spend a lesson with students grouped by their chosen type of texts, creating their own checklist for self and peer assessment. A blank checklist has been included in the 'Part Three: Additional Resources' section.
- Checking student learning journals to assess progress and understanding

SHARE

This is where students must take a risk and seek publication. It's a good idea to give suggestions of where students may seek publication for each form, but stress your valuing of independent investigation and originality of publication ideas. Encourage students to keep copies of any 'rejection' letters they receive because usually these will contain advice for future compositions as well as being a nice record of their attempt to be published.

At the end of the project, as a class, celebrate each individual's composition effort by having a 'Publish Me Picnic'. Have them bring in rugs and picnic food and take out a special 'author' chair for sharing favourite excerpts of compositions OR all of the short films and documentaries.

PART THREE
ADDITIONAL RESOURCES

A range of additional resources have been included to support you as you work through your first projects in English and then beyond as you begin designing your own projects. These additional resources include:

- The project design grid. This grid will help you decide on the hook lesson, product, audience and guest expert. When you become more confident with PBL, you may also like to give this to your students to design their own projects.
- Formative assessment strategies list. This brief list gives you an overview of some of the key formative assessment strategies that we use to help us track student learning throughout projects. Google is your friend with this resource — for each strategy you will find numerous resources online.
- Blank checklist. We love a checklist! They're awesome for peer and self-assessment. You or your students can modify this checklist.
- Project outline proforma. This document is essentially a blank slate for designing your own project. It gives you a sense of the key elements that should be included — the driving question plus the content/learning experiences relevant to each stage of learning (discover, create, share). Space has also been given to indicate formative assessment and due dates where applicable.
- Project Evaluation Checklist. This is for you to use to evaluate the projects you run with your students. Running through this handy list will help you to ensure that your students are participating in PBL, and not just 'doing a project'. Use this for EVERY project.
- Rubrics. Throughout the sample projects in this book, we have made reference to the use of assessment rubrics for helping students develop essential 21st-century skills such as collaboration, digital citizenship and critical and creative thinking. A number of these have been included here to support your students' development of the skills.

HOOK	EXPERT	PRODUCT	AUDIENCE
Model building	Academic	Video (draw my life/paper slide/Minecraft screencast)	Principal/HT/Teachers
Watching YouTube	Author	Documentary	Class within school
Drama activities	Director (film/theatre)	Film	Class in another school (face to face or online via Skype)
Taking students outside	Celebrity	Website (Weebly, wix)	Whole school
Garden health assessment and revamp	Engineer	Picture book	Grandparents
Tasting foods	Journalist	Novel/Novella	Local politician
Classroom cinema	Game designer	Book/eBook	Nursing home
Guest expert talk	Artist/Musician	Graphic novel	Preschool
6-word story/memoir/play	Business person	Exhibition	Online
Twitter Q&A with expert	Community clubs/Organisations	Food stall	Local/State library
Art – painting	Chef/Baker	Innovative design and prototype (loom band)	Local art gallery
Celebrity head/Match the pictures	Fashion designer	Video game design	University campus
Introductory video from expert	Politician	Poetry performance/Reading	Youth workers
Skype call with expert	Sportsperson	*Horrible Histories* episode	Expert (see other column)
Playing video games	Gardener	Interpretive dance	Parents and friends
Scavenger hunt	NGO representative	Stage performance	Charity representatives

FORMATIVE ASSESSMENT STRATEGIES

- Goals/Medals/Missions – daily, weekly or using a checklist for a draft
- Hexagonal thinking
- Star/Star/Wish
- Think/Puzzle/Explore
- Quizzes
- Traffic lights
- SOLO taxonomy
- Punk learner rubric
- Star-bursting
- 30 second check-in
- Exit tickets
- Rubrics for 21st century skills
- Blogging
- KWHL chart
- Rubrics for products
- Gallery walk
- Timed writing challenges

NAME:						
CRITERIA	TEACHER/PEER FEEDBACK			I USED FEEDBACK TO IMPROVE		
	STILL LEARNING	ACHIEVED	ABOVE & BEYOND	DIDN'T	TRIED	DID
1						
2						
3						
4						
5						
6						
7						
8						
9						
10						

MEDALS: (MAIN STRENGTHS)

MISSIONS: (IMPROVEMENTS NEEDED FOR THIS ESSAY)

PART THREE: ADDITIONAL RESOURCES

REPRODUCIBLE – ADDITIONAL RESOURCES

163

NOTE: As mentioned previously, one of the world's most reputable organisations in advocating quality Project Based Learning is The Buck Institute for Education. They share a wide range of very useful resources, and we are lucky enough to have been given permission to reproduce some of our favourites here for you in this book. The rubrics on the following pages and the 'Project Essentials Checklist' are the creation of the hard working and inspiring team at The Buck Institute for Education (www.bie.org).

PROJECT ESSENTIALS CHECKLIST

DOES THE PROJECT … ?	👍	👎	?
FOCUS ON SIGNIFICANT CONTENT AND AUTHENTIC ISSUES Students learn important subject matter content and address problems and issues from the world outside the classroom			
ORGANISE ACTIVITIES AROUND A DRIVING QUESTION OR CHALLENGE Students find the complex, open-ended question or challenge to be a meaningful focus for their work			
ESTABLISH A NEED TO KNOW AND DO Students are brought into the project by an entry event that captures interest and begins the inquiry process			
ENGAGE STUDENTS IN INQUIRY Students think deeply and ask further questions as they generate answers and solutions			
REQUIRE INNOVATION Students generate new answers and/or create unique products in response to the Driving Question or challenge			
DEVELOP 21ST-CENTURY SKILLS Students build critical & creative thinking, collaboration and presentation skills that are taught and assessed			
ENCOURAGE STUDENT VOICE AND CHOICE Students, with guidance from the teacher, make decisions that affect the course of the project			
INCORPORATE FEEDBACK AND REVISION Students use feedback to improve their work and create high-quality products			
CONCLUDE WITH A PUBLIC PRESENTATION Students exhibit products or present solutions, explain their work to others and respond to content- and process-focused questions			

REPRODUCIBLE – ADDITIONAL RESOURCES

CRITICAL THINKING RUBRIC FOR PBL

©2013 BUCK INSTITUTE FOR EDUCATION

CRITICAL THINKING OPPORTUNITY AT PHASES OF A PROJECT	BELOW STANDARD	APPROACHING STANDARD	AT STANDARD	ABOVE STANDARD ☐
LAUNCHING THE PROJECT: ANALYSE DRIVING QUESTION AND BEGIN INQUIRY	• I cannot explain what I would need to know to be able to answer the Driving Question • I still need to learn how another person might think differently about the Driving Question • I still need to learn how to ask questions about what our audience or product users might want or need	• I can identify a few things I would need to know to be able to answer the Driving Question • I can understand that another person might think differently about the Driving Question • I can ask a few questions about what our audience or product users might want or need	• I can explain what I would need to know to be able to answer the Driving Question • I can explain how different people might think about the Driving Question • I can ask lots of questions about what our audience or product users might want or need	
BUILDING KNOWLEDGE, UNDERSTANDING, AND SKILLS: GATHER AND EVALUATE INFORMATION	• I still need to learn how to use information from different sources to help answer the Driving Question • I still need to learn how to think about whether my information is relevant or if I have enough	• I can use information from different sources to help answer the Driving Question, but I may have trouble putting it together • I can think about whether my information is relevant and if I have enough, but I don't always decide carefully	• I can use information from different sources to help answer the Driving Question • I can decide if my information is relevant and if I have enough	
DEVELOPING AND REVISING IDEAS AND PRODUCTS: USE EVIDENCE AND CRITERIA	• I still need to learn how to identify the reasons and evidence an author or speaker uses to support a point • I still need to learn how to decide if an idea for a product or an answer to the Driving Question is a good one • I still need to learn how to use feedback from other students and adults to improve my writing or my design for a product	• I can identify some of the reasons and evidence an author or speaker uses to support a point • I can tell when an idea for a product or an answer to the Driving Question is a good one, but cannot always say why • I can sometimes use feedback from other students and adults to improve my writing or my design for a product	• I can explain how an author or speaker uses reasons and evidence to support a point that helps me answer the Driving Question • I can explain how to decide if an idea for a product or an answer to the Driving Question is a good one • I can use feedback from other students and adults to improve my writing or my design for a product	
PRESENTING PRODUCTS AND ANSWERS TO DRIVING QUESTION: JUSTIFY CHOICES	• I still need to learn how to explain my ideas in an order that makes sense • I still need to learn how to use appropriate facts or relevant details to support my ideas	• I can explain my ideas, but some might be in the wrong order • I can use some facts and details to support my ideas, but they are not always appropriate and relevant	• I can explain my ideas in an order that makes sense • I can use appropriate facts and relevant details to support my ideas	

COLLABORATION RUBRIC FOR PBL: INDIVIDUAL PERFORMANCE

©2013 BUCK INSTITUTE FOR EDUCATION

	BELOW STANDARD	APPROACHING STANDARD	AT STANDARD	ABOVE STANDARD
				☐
TAKES RESPONSIBILITY	<ul><li>I need to prepare for and join team discussions</li><li>I need reminders to do project work</li><li>My project work is not done on time</li><li>I need to learn how to use feedback from others</li></ul>	<ul><li>I am usually prepared for and join team discussions</li><li>I do some project work, but sometimes need to be reminded</li><li>I complete most project work on time</li><li>I sometimes use feedback from others</li></ul>	<ul><li>I am prepared for work with the team; I have studied required material and use it to explore ideas in discussions</li><li>I do project work without having to be reminded</li><li>I complete project work on time</li><li>I use feedback from others to improve my work</li></ul>	
HELPS THE TEAM	<ul><li>I need to cooperate with my team and help the team solve problems</li><li>I need to learn how to help make discussions effective</li><li>I need to learn how to give useful feedback to others</li><li>I need to learn to offer to help others if they need it</li></ul>	<ul><li>I cooperate with the team but do not help it solve problems</li><li>I usually help make discussions effective, but do not always follow the rules, ask enough questions or express ideas clearly</li><li>I give feedback to others, but it may not always be helpful</li><li>I sometimes offer to help others if they need it</li></ul>	<ul><li>I help the team solve problems and manage conflicts</li><li>I help make discussions effective by following agreed-upon rules, asking and answering questions, clearly expressing ideas</li><li>I give helpful feedback to others</li><li>I offer to help others do their work if needed</li></ul>	
RESPECTS OTHERS	<ul><li>I am sometimes impolite or unkind to teammates (may interrupt, ignore others' ideas, hurt feelings)</li><li>I need to learn how to listen to other points of view and disagree kindly</li></ul>	<ul><li>I am usually polite and kind to teammates</li><li>I usually listen to other points of view and disagree kindly</li></ul>	<ul><li>I am polite and kind to teammates</li><li>I listen to other points of view and disagree kindly</li></ul>	

PRESENTATION RUBRIC FOR PBL

©2013 BUCK INSTITUTE FOR EDUCATION

PROCESS

CRITICAL THINKING OPPORTUNITY AT PHASES OF A PROJECT	BELOW STANDARD	APPROACHING STANDARD	AT STANDARD	ABOVE STANDARD
EXPLANATION OF IDEAS & INFORMATION	• Uses inappropriate facts and irrelevant details to support main ideas	• Chooses some facts and details that support main ideas, but there may not be enough, or some are irrelevant	• Chooses appropriate facts and relevant, descriptive details to support main ideas and themes	☐
ORGANISATION	• Does not include everything required in presentation • Presents ideas in an order that does not make sense • Does not plan timing of presentation well; it is too short or too long	• Includes almost everything required in presentation • Tries to present ideas in an order, but it doesn't always makes sense • Presents for the right length of time, but some parts may be too short or too long	• Includes everything required in presentation • Presents ideas in an order that makes sense • Organises time well; no part of the presentation is rushed, too short or too long	
EYES & BODY	• Does not look at audience; reads notes • Fidgets or slouches a lot	• Makes some eye contact, but reads notes or slides most of the time • Fidgets or slouches a little	• Keeps eye contact with audience most of the time; only glances at notes or slides • Has a confident posture	
VOICE	• Speaks too quietly or not clearly • Does not speak appropriately for the situation (may be too informal or use slang)	• Speaks loudly and clearly most of the time • Speaks appropriately for the situation most of the time	• Speaks loudly and clearly • Speaks appropriately for the situation, using formal English when appropriate	
PRESENTATION AIDS	• Does not use audio/visual aids or media • Uses inappropriate or distracting audio/visual aids or media	• Uses audio/visual aids or media, but they sometimes distract from the presentation, or do not add to ideas and themes	• Uses well-produced audio/visual aids or media to add to main ideas and themes	
RESPONSE TO AUDIENCE QUESTIONS	• Does not answer audience questions	• Answers some audience questions, but not clearly or completely	• Answers audience questions clearly and completely	
PARTICIPATION IN TEAM PRESENTATIONS	• Not all team members participate; only one or two speak	• All team members participate, but not equally	• All team members participate for about the same length of time, and are able to answer questions	

CREATIVITY & INNOVATION RUBRIC FOR PBL

©2013 BUCK INSTITUTE FOR EDUCATION

PROCESS

CRITICAL THINKING OPPORTUNITY AT PHASES OF A PROJECT	BELOW STANDARD	APPROACHING STANDARD	AT STANDARD	ABOVE STANDARD
LAUNCHING THE PROJECT: DEFINE THE CREATIVE CHALLENGE	• I may just 'follow directions' without understanding why something needs to be created. • I still need to learn how to think about what people might need or like when they use or see what is created.	• I know that something needs to be created but cannot give detailed reasons why. • I have a basic idea of what people might need or like when they use or see what is created.	• I understand the reasons why something needs to be created. • I understand the needs and interests of the people who will use or see what is created.	☐
BUILDING KNOWLEDGE, UNDERSTANDING AND SKILLS: IDENTIFY SOURCES OF INFORMATION	• I use only the usual sources of information (website, book, article).	• I find one or two sources of information that are unusual.	• I find unusual ways to get information.	
DEVELOPING AND REVISING IDEAS AND PRODUCTS: GENERATE AND SELECT IDEAS	• I think of ideas for the product that are not new or original. • I pick an idea without deciding which one is best. • I still need to learn how to improve on the idea. • I still need to learn how to use feedback from others to improve written products.	• I think of some new ideas for the product. • I quickly decide which idea is best. • I might think about how to improve on the idea, but might not. • I use some feedback to make small changes in written products.	• I think of many new ideas for the product. • I carefully decide which idea is best. • I ask new questions and think about how to improve on the idea. • I use feedback from others to improve written products.	
PRESENTING PRODUCTS AND ANSWERS TO DRIVING QUESTION: PRESENT WORK TO USERS/TARGET AUDIENCE	• I present ideas and products in just the regular ways (show PowerPoint slides, read notes, have no audience involvement).	• I try to add some interesting touches to visual aids but they may not add much, or they may be distracting. • I try to involve the audience actively in the presentation but it is very quick or does not work well.	• I create visual aids that are interesting to see and hear. • I involve the audience actively in the presentation (ask them questions, have them do an activity).	

Continued...

CREATIVITY & INNOVATION RUBRIC FOR PBL (CONTINUED...)

©2013 BUCK INSTITUTE FOR EDUCATION

PRODUCT

	BELOW STANDARD	APPROACHING STANDARD	AT STANDARD	ABOVE STANDARD
ORIGINALITY	• My product looks like things that have been seen before; it is not new or unique.	• My product has some new ideas, but it still looks mostly like things that have been seen before.	• My product is new, unique, surprising; shows a personal touch.	☐
VALUE	• My product is not useful or valuable by the people who use or see it. • My product would not work in the real world.	• My product is somewhat useful but it may not exactly meet the needs of people who use or see it. • My product might work in the real world, but might have problems.	• My product is seen as useful and valuable by the people who use or see it. • My product would work in the real world (not too hard, expensive, time-consuming to create).	
STYLE	• My product looks like other things like this; it is made in a traditional style. • My product has several pieces that do not fit together; it is a mish-mash.	• My product has some interesting touches. • My product has some pieces that may be too much or do not fit together well.	• My product is well-made, impressive, designed with style. • My product's pieces all go well together.	